Applying

to

LAW
SCHOOL

*a guide for
the rest of us*

J.D. MILLER

Produced and edited by J.D. Miller

Cover graphics and formatting provided by Streetlight Graphics (streetlightgraphics.com)

ISBN-13: 978-0-9850070-0-3

CONTENTS

PREFACE
SO YOU ARE THINKING OF APPLYING TO LAW SCHOOL

HELLO, POTENTIAL LAW student! Thank you for taking a moment to flip through this tome of information and guidance on the art of applying to law school. Since you now have the opportunity to peruse this preface before deciding to purchase, I thought it only right that I take this opportunity to introduce myself and explain a little bit about who I am and why I am doing this. As an added incentive, I will also provide you with the fundamental theorem of law school happiness.

Special Note: You will want to read to the end. I put the theorem at the end.

This is my clever way of making you read the whole chapter. Of course now that I have said it is at the end, you are far more likely to scroll down or flip through rather that read all of the important information that I am putting between here and there. Don't do that. In this book, as in life, the important stuff is in the details. Have some patience and read the whole thing.

Okay, so now that we have gotten that out of the way. Let me tell you a little bit about me: your humble author and learned guide through the thorny application process.

I am thirty-three years old and a 2006 graduate of Vermont Law School. I studied for and passed the Virginia Bar Exam in the summer of 2006 and I worked for one year as a document reviewer for legal temp agencies in the Washington, D.C. area while grinding through the hiring process for the federal government. I also provided pro bono services to local non-profit organizations in the northern Virginia area. Since 2007, I have been working for the federal government in an interesting, fulfilling, and legally relevant but non-lawyer position ever since.

Upon graduating from law school, I received two awards for excellence in various aspects of my academic studies, a beautiful diploma suitable for framing, and a bill for $130,000.00 in student loans.

I mention the student loan money only because it is important to know if you are going to understand why I wrote this book. I could pretend that it is nostalgia for my time in school or my desire to help others master the same path that I once travelled. But to be completely honest, I am not driven by an altruistic impulse to help you join an overly glutted legal labor market that already has too many lawyers, too few jobs, and a penchant for eating its young. Sure, helping people out is nice, but the long answer made short is that I need the money. I will go into this in greater detail later, but I want you to know that I am writing this book because I want you to buy this book, and I want you to buy this book because, quite simply, my student loans are *killing* me.

Not that this means the information I have is any less valid or applicable to you. In fact, I dare say it is more applicable because I learned the hard way how to make law school affordable. You, potential student, are the lucky recipient of this knowledge. I can tell you how to avoid making the same mistakes I did...or at least I can warn you now so you can see these potential pitfalls when they approach. At a minimum, I can help you decide whether or not law school is even something you should be considering.

My profit motivation insures for you my most brutal honesty, my most thorough explanations, and my most independent analysis. I don't want you to just buy this book. I want you to buy this book, and then I want you to love this book. I want you to buy this book, love this book, and ultimately I want you to *recommend* this book. I want you to come home for winter break during your first year of law school, and when your Aunt Gertrude pushes your cousin in front of you and asks you for advice on how little Stewie can go to law school some day, I want you to smile benevolently and say, "Law school is great, Stu! You're going to love it. Now, the first thing you do is you get this book, *Applying to Law School...*"

How this Book Is Organized

This book is informally divided into roughly four sections. I did not intend that when I was writing, but the chapters evolved naturally that way. For those of you who have read through the book once, I have also included a comprehensive Table of Contents to assist you in jumping from chapter to chapter and section to section as you proceed through your application process.

We begin our journey together with an introspective analysis of your motivations for applying to law school and we examine whether or not law school is a good fit for your personality and interests. I provide you with a series of five basic questions that every potential applicant should attempt to answer honestly before applying. Law school is not for everyone. If it is not for you then the sooner you realize it, the better.

We then take a detailed look at the application timeline and how you, the applicant, can fit into it. We discuss the Law School Admissions Test and how to prepare for it as well as how to interpret your score once you have taken the test. Finally, we look at all the various parts of your application to get a sense of the schools for which you are competitive – not just for admission but for scholarships as well.

The third section covers the actual application process. We discuss visiting schools and what to look for when evaluating a campus. We look at how to rank your pool of potential schools so that the best candidates for you naturally rise to the top of the list. We also take a close look at the reasons why financing your law school education through student loans is no longer always the smart investment decision that it used to be considered.

The final section covers the actual mechanics of applying to law school. We examine everything from preparing personal essays to chasing down the perfect recommendation letter. Finally, we discuss how to balance the cost versus the quality of your various law school choices. The goal of this book is to help applicants find the perfect school at the perfect price for each and every one of them.

Takeaways

Scattered throughout the chapters will be small highlighted nuggets labeled *Takeaways*. If you are rushing through the book to get to the good parts, make sure you stop to read the Takeaway. In each one, I try to condense the most fundamental rules of the section into only a sentence or two.

After you have read the takeaway and allowed the zeitgeist of what I am telling you to permeate through to your brain, come back and read the whole chapter again. You will get more out of it, I promise.

A Few Terms with Which You Should Be Familiar

There are a few terms with which you need to be familiar if you are going to have the basic vocabulary necessary to apply to law school. Most people read these terms for the first time and either make up their best guess at what they mean or run to the internet to look them up. You are reading this book. That makes you smart.

Application Package—The average law school application package consists of a school-specific application, an LSAT score, transcripts from previous institutions, and two or more recommendation letters. It should go without saying that the average applicant consists of much more.

CAS Report—Also known as the Credential Assembly Report. This is what the LSAC sends to your chosen law schools. It is the compilation of your LSAT score, transcripts, and recommendations. You will need to purchase a CAS Report for each school to which you apply.

FAFSA—The Free Application for Federal Student

Aid. The FAFSA is the form you fill out every year from the Department of Education that provides you with eligibility for federal student loans. Together with your taxes and each school's financial aid application, the FAFSA is a critical component of your financial aid package.

Juris Doctorate—also known as the J.D. or the Juris Doctor, this is the degree you get when you graduate from law school.

LSAT—The LSAT is short for the Law School Admissions Test. It is a standardized exam given globally to anyone interested in attending law school. No reputable law school will accept applicants without a LSAT score. Strangely enough, the LSAT is scored on a range of 120 points to 180 points.

LSAC—The LSAC is short for the Law School Admissions Council. The LSAC is both the administrator of the LSAT as well as a clearinghouse for many other aspects of the application package. The LSAC is a self-created middle-man monopoly. If you want to go to law school in the United States of America, you simply must deal with the LSAC.

U.S. News Rankings—Formerly known as the U.S. News and World Report rankings, the U.S. News rankings compile data from every law school such as average LSAT and GPA numbers, post-graduation employment rates, and bar passage rates. Using this data, law schools are ranked based on their supposed quality. There are other rankings out there but the U.S. News Rankings remains the 500lb gorilla.

Revealed: The Fundamental Theorem of Law School Happiness!

So here we are. Only a few pages into the book and I am already giving away the store. I promised I would give you the fundamental theorem of law school happiness and here it is:

$$(A / B) \times C = \text{Happy Law Student}$$

A-ha! Simple, right? No doubt you are saying to yourself, "Eureka! Finally I see! It is so easy!"

Yeah, right. Do not worry. There is more to it. Read on...

In this equation:

"A" equals the sum total of the applicant's parts including grades, essays, LSAT score, and ability to perform at the level required for the study of law. In short, A = You. Unless you have a self-confidence problem, I would treat this as a constant.

"B" equals the sum total of the parts of a particular law school in which the applicant is interested. This includes the school's average numbers for the LSAT and GPA as well as the school's bar passage rate, overall ranking, and reputation. More importantly, this also includes the applicant's emotional connection to the school based on exposure (visits, alumni meetings, etc.)

"C" equals the financial aid and scholarship package available to the student.

So that is the theorem. Assign numeric values to the variables and chart how each law school you are considering compares to one another. The lower the value, the better the school for you. The theorem is actually not that complicated and it does really work but only in that, "If I only knew then what I know now" sort of way. The hardest part of applying it is getting out of your own way.

Successfully applying to law school requires that you think of the process as a three-legged stool. One leg is the quality of the school. The second leg is your emotional connection to the school. If you prefer, you can think of this as representing how happy you would be to attend the school. The third leg is the financial aid package you are offered. At the top, where the seat of the stool is located, is where you sit: happily pursuing your Juris Doctorate at a good school that is not burying you in student loan debt.

Look, go ahead and buy the book. If you are seriously considering applying to law school, then I promise it is worth your time. For those of you who have already laid down your hard-earned money, thank you and please turn the page. We begin our journey with a few statistics designed to help anchor your decision-making in reality.

A FEW STATISTICS OF CONCERN

FACT

According to the ABA's website: In the 2011-2012 academic year, there are over 150,000 law students currently attending over 200 law schools throughout the United States. Fifty years ago, there were less than 140 law schools and class sizes were significantly smaller.

FACT

The average amount borrowed in academic year 2009-2010 (last available year) was $68,827...for a public law school. Those attending a private law school borrowed an average of $106,249.

FACT

From 2000 to 2010, borrowing costs have increased by $20,000 for public law schools and just under $40,000 for private law schools.

FACT

According to SimplyHired.com, the average salary for

an entry-level attorney is $53,000.

By my math, that works out to roughly $3,300 per month after taxes. If you went to a private law school (the majority of law schools are private) and you assume the best-case scenario that $85,000 of your debt is federal Direct Loans that you then consolidate through the thirty year repayment program, you will only have $21,249 in private loans. These are almost always set at a maximum of a ten year repayment plan. A Rough estimate of your monthly student loan bill is $850.00 for the next ten years and a little over $500.00 for the next twenty years after that.

The statistics for average salary do not consider individuals who are unemployed, under-employed, or employed in non-legal fields.

FACT

According to LawCrossing.com: In 2010, there were 26,239 attorney positions available for entry-level attorneys. Yet at the same time, 53,000 people took the bar exam.

FACT

You cannot discharge student loan debt through bankruptcy. Like a clichéd barbwire tattoo you get around your bicep one drunken spring break night, you are stuck with this debt forever.

FACT

Your dear author graduated in 2006 with over $130,000 in student loan debt. This debt load was *despite* a partial scholarship, work-study, and a full-time job as a Emergency Medical Technician at the local ambulance squad. My monthly student loan payments exceed $1,000.00 per month.

FACT

Unless I win the lottery or 100,000 of you promising young applicants buy this book, I will still be making this payment when both of my children are out of college.

FACT

The dramatic increase in the number of law schools *combined* with the ease of borrowing money to attend these law schools means that the difficulty in obtaining a law school education has plummeted. Unfortunately for all of us, it also means there are a lot of unqualified people out there going to law school who stand no chance of passing the bar in any state.

FACT

The market for graduates of good law schools who have passed the bar exam remains unchanged. If you truly want to be an attorney, there is good, fulfilling work out there for you. You are just going to have to fight your way to the front of an ever-growing field of yokels to make sure you are seen.

Takeaway:

In the last decade, the value of a law degree has dropped significantly while the cost of acquiring it has risen substantially. If you want the degree because it means financial security, you are better off becoming an ASE-certified mechanic. If you want to practice the law because you feel called to the profession, than read on because it is still totally worth it.

CHAPTER ONE
WHAT DO YOU WANT TO DO WITH YOUR LIFE?

W HAT DO YOU want to do with your life? It is the ultimate question, isn't it? For a lucky few, they either know from the beginning or they discover early on what they were meant to do with their lives. However, for the vast majority of people it is a long and arduous process of trial and error, and they go down one path only to stop, turn around, and head down another.

Personal Experience: Your Author's Law School Decision-Making Process

When I was a kid, I wanted to be an architect. Actually, to be completely honest, I wanted to be Wonder Woman—but mostly because I loved the idea of an invisible jet. Later, I wanted to be an astronaut followed almost immediately by a desire to be a pilot in an F-14 Tomcat (My Lord, I loved Top Gun). As the years passed, I toyed with the idea of being a race car driver, the smallest lineman in professional football, a

Jesuit priest, a presidential speech writer, and a physicist. I had all these grand dreams, these great ideas and even if you had asked me then, I would have been able to tell you that the one thing all my desires had in common was that I wanted to do something that mattered. If you had really pressed me on the issue, I would have told you that I wanted to be a cop.

I have always loved the idea of being a police officer. In my imagination as a young man, a police officer was always big and tough and worked an adventurous job keeping the rest of us safe. On their days off, police officers hung out with their friends, drank beer, and played video games. What wasn't to love? Police officers had fun, made a decent living, and got to be heroes every day.

So, upon graduating from high school, I proudly stepped out onto the road of adulthood and did...absolutely nothing.

Well, that is not entirely true. I went through the same panicked process of taking the SATs and applying to colleges that every middle-class high school student goes through. I had made decent grades and scored well enough on the SATs, but I never found a school where I thought I would be happy.

I tried a variety of jobs. I laid brick and built decks for awhile, but once I had mastered the fundamentals of construction, I grew bored. I joined the military but knew almost immediately that I was not going to make it a career. I scalped tickets and hawked t-shirts at concerts. I worked for a catering company and learned how to make teeny-tiny little hamburgers for wedding receptions. I painted houses. I worked on a farm and baled hay.

Basically, I dabbled for about seven years. I played around a bit over here and a bit over there learning a little about a lot of things but never quite settling into a career. Finally, I ended up back in my home state of North Carolina taking a couple of classes every semester to complete my Bachelor's degree and working three different jobs to make ends meet.

It would be nice to say I finally had an epiphany. I would love to be able to tell you that there was some instrumental episode in my past when I was exposed to the legal system and I realized my calling to be the next Earl Warren. Unfortunately, it is not the truth. The reality is that I woke up in 2002 and realized I was twenty-four years old and about to graduate from college with absolutely no idea what to do next. I was married to a crazy young lady just as aimless and lost as I was. We spent most of our time caretaking our landlord's farm and keeping a couple of horses and dogs. She worked as a low level functionary at a pharmaceutical research company while nurturing dreams of medical school. The highlight of our week was the Saturday night marathon session of video games on the Play Station 2. There was no moment of epiphany for me. I simply decided that the time was about right for me to find a respectable career.

I decided that my dreams of becoming a standup comedian or a famous actor or the next Stephen King were just that—dreams. I decided, in short, that I needed to accept the reality of my life and pursue the one reasonable avenue of professional success and personal satisfaction that was both appealing to me and available. I decided to return to my boyhood dream and become a cop.

I went home and told my wife that I was going to apply to the local police department. My pronouncement heralded the beginning of an epic fight that ended only when a new fight began over which one of us was going to be more of a martyr and sleep on the couch. My wife ended up sleeping on the couch and I, unwilling to cede the point, slept in the bed of my 1991 pickup truck. Nobody slept in the bed that night except our dog—which had intelligently chosen to abstain from making any decision over competing loyalties.

My wife stated her point quite emphatically: She did not want to be married to a police officer. She still had grand dreams of becoming a famous epidemiologist or veterinarian or vascular surgeon or whatever the hell she wanted to be that week, and she was not quite ready to reconcile her dreams with the fact that her husband wanted to be "just" a beat cop.

I did not actually blame her. It is true to say that picking a career is, in many ways, a life-limiting decision. It is essentially the first truly adult decision you make. Some people are ready to make the decision as soon as they are old enough to talk and others are pushing into their fifties and still have not been able to face up to it. Don't get me wrong. I am not taking anything away from the thirty-eight year old sales associate at AutoZone or the forty-two year old barista-slash-manager at the local Starbucks. Making the decision of what you want to do with your life is a big deal, and the right time to face it is different for everyone.

Knowing what I know now, I am glad I waited as long as I did. After all, I was essentially saying:

> "Hello, World. This is me and this is what I want to do. I am pretty sure that this is how I want to define myself in my lifetime. This is the intersection where my talents and capabilities meet my hopes and dreams. Some people may be richer than me and some others may be

smarter and some may go on to do amazing things for which they will be remembered forever, but this is where I fit into the grand scheme of things."

Of course, it is important to remember that it is never impossible to change career paths or go on to do great things—it is just bloody difficult sometimes.

So, after a terrible night's sleep and a classic day of reflection while I sat staring at a pond, I decided that I did not want to make a decision at all. The way I saw it, applying to law school might be the way for me to postpone this "life-limiting" decision for at least a few years. If I had made up a pros and cons list (and I think I might have done just that at some point), it would have read something like this:

Pros:

— I will obtain a professional degree and thus enhanced career prospects.
— I will avoid making a career decision for another three years.
— I like to argue.
— I can move somewhere new.
— I am not precluded from returning to any of my previous interests.
— I can still become a cop and I can even apply to the FBI.

Cons:

— I don't particularly care about being a lawyer.
— I am already twenty-four years old. I will not begin a "real job" until I'm almost thirty.
— I will need to borrow student loans to finance my education.

After adding up the pros and subtracting the cons, I decided law school was the place for me.

Yes, my decision was just that cavalier.

Shame on me. I did not know any better. I knew law school was competitive, but I did not know how competitive. I knew law school was arduous, but I could not conceive how arduous. I knew law school was expensive, but I did not have any idea what the cost would truly be. You are already one step ahead of me because you bought this book. You get to benefit from my past mistakes. Lucky you!

You Only Need a Law Degree if You Want to Be a Lawyer

I am a firm believer in learning from experience. For example, after a careful examination of my experience, I can tell you that my primary motivation for going to law school was avoiding another fight with my wife and forestalling the decision of what I was actually going to do with myself for as long as possible.

Now, I got lucky. Law school worked out for me. I use my degree all the time and I derive a great deal of fulfillment from my career. There is no guarantee you will be so lucky. In fact, the odds are against it. Let me tell you a well known but rarely spoken fact:

> *A law degree is not really necessary for any career path other than being a practicing attorney. While a law degree can help get your foot in the door of many careers, having experience gained from other jobs or internships can be just as effective...and it can also be far less expensive in the long run.*

I did not know that little truth at the time. I chose to get a law degree and, as a result, I have a great job that I was already qualified for anyway and $130,000 in student loan debt. Yea for me.

How Do You Know What Is Right for You?

To be honest, I have no idea. Remember, I am the guy who bounced from job to job until he was in his late twenties. However, if you want my advice, then please read on:

If you are feeling particularly spiritual, then I will tell you that the short answer is to pause for a moment and try to hear what your inner voice has to say. For me, I recognized that the unifying theme of all my professional desires as a child centered on a desire to help my fellow man and to see justice prevail over injustice. Saying I wanted to be a cop was just a way of putting a label on that desire to do something meaningful and valuable to society.

Take a moment and close your eyes. Think back to your childhood. Think back to the games you played and the daydreams you had. When you were a child what did you want to be? Think about all the different ways you answered that question. Is there a unifying theme? Is there something that unites them all? If so, that just might be your answer.

If you are looking for a slightly more logical approach, then I would recommend you take one or more of the professional aptitude and personality tests offered to employment-seeking professionals. Take the Briggs-Meyers personality assessment. Take the military's ASVAB. See what else is out there. Learn where your aptitude is strongest and then apply that

to your childhood ideas of what you wanted to do with
your life.

Takeaway:

A law degree is unnecessary for any job other being
an attorney. It is now also so unbelievably expensive
that it is rarely worth getting the degree unless you
know in your heart of hearts that you want to be an
attorney. Figuring out what you do and do not want to
do with your life ahead of time can save you a ton of
money and heartburn down to the road.

CHAPTER TWO
IS APPLYING TO LAW SCHOOL RIGHT FOR YOU?

W^{E HAVE COVERED} how to figure out what you want to do with your life. Those of you who have decided that life is better spent in the fields of medicine, engineering, or professional jai alai have already closed this book and moved on to bigger and better things. Peace, you fine folks. We will miss you and we wish you the best of luck.

Now, what about the rest of you who are still thinking that law school might be something in which you are interested? Do you actually have any idea what being a lawyer means? Do you know what law school will require of you? Do you have the skills? The talent? In short, do you have any idea whether or not you can succeed at law school?

When I was a younger man, I became a passionate fan of triathlons. I have watched the Ironman Championships on television every year since the mid-nineties, and I follow the career trajectory of ultra-endurance athletes the way other men follow their favorite quarterbacks. I even, for a while, thought I might have what it takes to be a professional long distance triathlete. That is, until I signed up for my first race.

I am short in stature where these triathletes are tall. I am stocky where they are rail thin. I swim like a bull moose wading a river and I ride a bike like a grizzly bear on a unicycle. I also really enjoy a fine cigar a little more than I should and I have been known to engage in the occasional alcoholic libation. The unfortunate reality is that I am simply not physically capable of competing in the sport of triathlon and there is no amount of training, dedication, or skill that is going to change that. It only took a few races to disabuse me of the notion that I was going to be making my living racing across the Hawaiian lava flows. While I still enjoy participating in triathlons, I have learned to let go of my dream of being on a box of Wheaties.

Law school is a lot like a triathlon. It is a mix of a variety of different disciplines which almost anyone can do but few can do extremely well. It requires endurance and dedication and a willingness to engage in disciplined work with no short-term potential for immediate gratification. Law school, like an Ironman triathlon, is all about grinding it out seemingly forever with the hope of a big reward at the end.

Five Questions

So, here is where I am going to ask you to do a quick self-assessment and decide if you have what it takes to succeed at the long distance triathlon that is the law school experience. Follow me through this series of five questions and try to be as honest as you can when answering them. In the end, after all, you are only deceiving yourself if you don't.

Question 1:

Have you graduated from high school and have you graduated from college or intend to graduate from college in the next two years?

If you answer yes, please move on. If no, then please close this book and focus on the academic program in front of you. Come back to this book when you are a little further along.

Question 2:

Can you read?

Now, before you burn a short, stocky effigy of me for asking such an offensive question, allow me to expound on what I mean. When I ask,—'Can you read?'—I don't just mean can you read a book or read the local paper. What I mean is: can you read with a strong sense of critical comprehension? Can you parse a text and understand both what the author is saying and not saying? Can you read quickly and concisely? Do you have a larger than average vocabulary? Do you read literature for fun and fulfillment?

Look, a lot of law school guides are going to gloss over the fact that being a good reader is fundamental to law school. They are going to talk about all the non-reading undergraduate engineers and science majors who make great law students (here is a hint: they are still great readers). They're going to offer a variety of exercises and practical methodologies to help the weak reader become better. They are going to talk about visual versus tactile and auditory learners, and they are going to offer tips to improve comprehension and focus.

I am going to call it all horse crap.

However, if you think it can help you then by all means go forth and conquer. I think that is great and I wish you the best of luck. I am still going to call it horse crap.

Takeaway:

You need to be a good reader to handle law school. You need to be a great reader to succeed in law school.

If you are not already a good reader by the time you apply, you are not going to have the basic skills necessary to learn to be a good *legal* reader. A good legal reader can chew through a dense legal text and tease out the relevant facts in just a few moments. A great legal reader can also find the legal theory being applied in the same amount of time. Skillful reading is not just a nice skill to have. It is absolutely necessary.

If you are not a good reader at this point, I am not going to tell you that you cannot survive law school. You can, but it is going to be very difficult. There are a variety of exercises and alternative methods to help mitigate this deficiency. I strongly recommend you explore those options and determine whether getting a law degree is going to be worth the struggle for you.

Question 3:

Can you write?

Please put down the torches and see the first paragraph of Question 2.

Writing is the yin to reading's yang. Writing is how an attorney expresses himself or herself. Writing is the physical manifestation of an attorney's kung fu. Sure, movies and television shows like to focus on the great oral arguments, the carefully crafted cross examinations, and the sensational closing summations, but the real skill of any attorney is in his writing.

A well-written letter stuns your opponent. A well-written brief musters the law to your side and predisposes the judges to favor you. A well-written judgment can stand the test of time and social change and make you immortal.

Go read *Marbury v. Madison.* Over two hundred years later and it is still a masterpiece of judicial writing that carved out the independence and power of the American judiciary just as effectively as the U.S. Constitution had for the executive and legislative branches of the government. After that, go read *Dred Scott v. Sanford.* A horrible decision so powerfully written that it stymied the abolitionist movement until the outbreak of the Civil War seven years later.

The citation for *Marbury v. Madison,* by the way, is 5 U.S. 137 (1803) and *Dred Scott v. Sandford* is 60 U.S. 393 (1857). Don't worry about what the numbers mean. You will learn how to find and cite cases when you take your first year legal writing class. For now, just type both cases into Google and read them online. If the language seems archaic, try reading them aloud. There is powerful magic in the words.

Takeaway:

Good writing has the power to change minds. At the very least, you must have a competent command of grammar, spelling, punctuation, and sentence structure before you even think of applying to law school.

As with reading, I am not going to tell you that you cannot survive law school if you are not an excellent writer. I am going to tell you that you are going to have a very difficult time of it and should definitely consider if law school is worth it. If you have any doubts, go buy a copy of the New York Times and pick an opinion piece at random. Read it and decide if you agree or disagree. Now, go write at least seven hundred words to the editor advocating your position. Don't worry. We will wait.

All finished? Good.

If that took you longer than two hours, you need to work on your writing. If that took you less than two hours, you are probably fine. If that took you less than an hour, then you are golden. Congrats.

Question 4:

Have you ever been convicted of a crime?

This is not a deal breaker. In fact, there was a convicted murderer who was applying to sit for the bar when I was going through law school. Other convicted felons who have been able to demonstrate their rehabilitation frequently sit for various state bars. Still, be aware that you will need to disclose any criminal activity—no matter how stupid and juvenile— during the application process (I will talk more about this later) and again when you apply to sit for your state's bar. The failure to disclose is far worse than whatever it is you did as a freshman that you are afraid to admit on your application.

Question 5:

Can you work hard?

There is one adage I heard repeatedly in law school: "You get out of it what you put into it." I think it is true enough that I am repeating it here and asking you to believe it like I do. This does not mean that you should join the various social clubs and intramural kickball teams that every law school offers. It also does not mean that you should choose to spend every moment of your free time volunteering at the legal aid clinic.

These are, of course, perfectly wonderful and valuable ways to round out three years of legal education, but they are not what is meant when your professors tell you that law school is what you make of it. A little known reality of law school is the following: if you can survive the first month of the first semester without your head exploding, most likely you will be able to survive all three years of law school.

This is because the first month of school is when you will learn how to brief cases and prepare for the class lectures and even write summaries and model motions. Your professors will use that first month just to make sure there are not any complete knuckle-draggers in the back of the room whose inability to grasp the intricacies of modern tort or contract law will inevitably degrade the learning of all the other students. After that, they will pretty much let you slide until exam time and then your entire grade will be made up of the final exam...which is usually submitted using one of several double-blind methods. The smart, hard working students will get the A's and B+'s while the bulk of the students will get B's and B-'s and a few stragglers in the back will get C+'s or C's depending on the school's grade curve..

No one will get lower than a C unless they write something obscene about the professor's mother on their blue exam book or otherwise intentionally shoot themselves in the foot.

I want to repeat this because it is really important:

No one who actually makes some measurable effort on the exam will get lower than a C/C+.

Takeaway:

After the first semester, it is almost impossible to fail out of law school. While I'm sure there are a few individuals every semester who find a way, if you show up to class and buy the text book, you are going to pass the class.

Personal Experience: Learning from Your Author's Mistakes (Part 1)

My wife and I decided to divorce during my second year of law school. More truthfully, she moved out of our apartment one early spring day at the beginning of the second semester and took all of our furniture and our dog with her. I spent the rest of the semester and all of the summer going through the mandatory separation period before filing for divorce. To say that it was an emotionally trying experience would be an understatement. It was hellish. My point in telling you this, however, is not to recreate the cathartic experience of getting over my ex-wife. It is to tell you that I essentially shut down during the second semester of my 2L year and yet still passed my courses.

When I say I shut down, I mean I really shut down. I mailed it in. I was an empty suit. I hung a "Gone Fishin'" sign on the end of my nose. I withdrew completely.

I remember going into each one of my classes (my two most important that semester were Evidence and Estates) and telling the professors in each that I was dealing with some personal problems. I promised that

I would be present in class each day, but I warned them that they should not expect me to be prepared to *ever* discuss the material. All my professors looked at me sympathetically, nodded their heads, and mentally checked me off their student rosters. It was no skin off their backs whether I was prepared or not. I would either pass the exams at the end of the semester or I would not.

I came out of my stupor about two weeks before the end of the semester rolled around. I had not read a single case. I had not taken any notes. I knew I was in trouble but I also knew that I did not really have much of a choice about my options—I could either sink or swim. I locked myself in my empty apartment, and I spent two days straight reviewing the course syllabi and briefing the cases my professors had listed. I used the commercial course outlines for both Evidence and Estates, and I used every study technique I had ever learned to recreate the material in a dozen different ways. I recorded my own voice. I created flash cards. I wrote outline after outline of the evolution of the law for each class until I could condense it onto a single page of cryptic shorthand.

It was an epic cram session and, to be completely honest, it almost drove me insane. At the end of it, however, I stumbled into that lecture hall smelling of B.O., cigarettes, and frozen pizza, and scored three B+'s, a C+ and a C. I finished the semester with a 2.71 semester average.

Let me put this more simply. I did nothing but sleep in the back of the classroom for an entire semester of law school and I still managed to score a B- average.

That Vast and Comfortable Space between Failure and Success

So, what does this have to do with whether or not you can work hard?

Now that you know law school is not something you can easily fail once you get past the first semester, I hope you also realize that it is incredibly easy to fall somewhere in that vast and comfortable space between failing out and succeeding. It is where the bulk of law students spend at least some of their time. They are not doing poorly and they are not doing great. They are treading water and learning just enough about each case to regurgitate the high points to the professor without getting nailed with a trick question.

It is an easy place to be. It is a comfortable place to be. It is absolutely NOT where you want to be. The law students who surf their way through three years of law school in this manner do themselves a grave injustice. They also have great difficulty passing the bar.

Law school is a unique opportunity to learn and discuss the law in an environment that will never be created for you again in your entire career. Guided by a learned professor and surrounded by your peers, you have the opportunity to wrestle with the law, to challenge assumptions, and recreate the evolution of legal theory. Once you begin to comprehend it, you will quickly see that the law can be something awe inspiring.

You should approach every class like the expenditure of a finite resource that can never be replaced. You will never have another opportunity to learn the law in this way again, and I promise you that the lectures you engage in and the briefs you prepare during law school will form the cornerstone of your professional practice for the rest of your career.

If I have one regret, it is that I wasted an entire

semester of school dealing with the end of my marriage. Sure, it was incredibly painful at the time, but I am still more pissed that I hurt my cumulative grade point average with a crappy semester. As I grow older, I am even more disappointed that I lost the opportunity to engage in a semester's worth of debate. I regret that I lost the chance to really learn. That gap has an impact and even today my weakest area of knowledge is in the area of estate planning.

Thus, my question: Can you work hard? Can you grab law school around the middle and squeeze every last drop of value out of it? Can you maximize your investment in time, energy, and debilitating student loans so that you emerge from three years of school with a mind sharpened to a razor's edge by Socratic debate, steeped in the case law of the United States, and ready to ace your chosen state's bar exam?

If so, follow me into the next chapter and we will discuss the importance of owning a calendar.

CHAPTER THREE
THE LAW SCHOOL APPLICATION TIMELINE

WELCOME TO THE practical side of applying to law school. You have, no doubt, spent the last few days carefully mulling your answers to the five questions I posed to you in Chapter Two and you have decided that you are ready to make the commitment. In fact, you are sick and tired of hearing me wax poetic about law school and you are ready for some of that nifty first-hand advice for which you have already plunked down your hard earned money when you bought this book.

Right. Let it never be said that I do not sing for my supper. Without further ado, here is my first piece of tangible advice:

Get a calendar.

Yup. That's right. I just blew your hair back, didn't I?

Of course, I mean a lot more than just get a calendar. What I really mean is that it is time to start structuring your law school application timeline. It is time to mesh the requirements of the application process with your own internal timeline of life. Some of the questions you need to ask:

— When are applications available?
— When's the next LSAT date?
— When do you intend to graduate?
— Do you plan to take a major vacation after graduation? Any plans to tour Europe or hike the Appalachian Trail that would affect you availability to start school on time?
— What about a significant other? Are you planning on incorporating his or her timeline into your own?

There's not much I can do to help you with your own personal calendar, but I can give you a clear sense of what the law school timeline is like. It will be up to you to figure out when the best time for you is to jump in.

I want you to imagine if the Indianapolis 500 was held on the same road and at the same time as your regular morning commute. Trying to merge into traffic on the day of the race would be a lot like the law school application process. Imagine hundreds of cars whipping around turn after turn in a tight pack. Now imagine yourself pulling onto the on-ramp in a 1982 Honda Civic. Now imagine stomping on the gas and trying to merge into that mess.

Do you have that image in your mind? Good. That is applying to law school. If you are prepared and ready, it will be a reasonably neat and seamless process in which your personal calendar and the law school application calendar will line up perfectly. You will easily transition from your previous background to your new job as a first year student.

If you are unprepared or just plain unlucky, it will be a metaphorical multiple vehicle pile-up that will force you to wait another year or to submit hurried and poorly drafted applications, bad LSAT scores, and late financial aid applications which will knock you off balance and diminish your opportunities before you ever even get the chance to make it into the classroom.

Personal Experience: Learning from Your Author's Mistakes (Part 2)

I made the decision to go to law school for three main reasons: First, it avoided the fight with my wife over my desire to be a police officer. Second, I thought it would give me eligibility I did not otherwise possess to apply to the FBI. Third, it allowed me to delay for at least three years the need to make a final decision about what to do with my life.

I made my decision to apply sometime in the middle of the spring semester of my final year in college. Having no idea what the law school application process was like; I immediately jumped on the internet and printed off the applications for a couple of different schools that I liked. I also grabbed a few applications for schools that were located in really nice places. I mean, who would not want to go to law school in Hawaii?

Because my wife was from a little town just outside of Boston and because she was so desperate to get back to New England, I decided I would really focus my applications on the Boston area. With that in mind, I grabbed applications for the following schools:

01. Harvard
02. Boston College
03. Boston University
04. Northeastern University
05. Suffolk University

06. Stanford
07. U. Cal—Berkeley
08. UNC—Chapel Hill
09. Duke University
10. University of Hawaii

I thought ten would be a nice round number. I had Hawaii on the list because I have always thought Hawaii was beautiful and I would love to live there. I added the two California schools because I visited San Francisco once and really liked it out there as well. I also made sure that I added every major school in the Boston area. I even chose Suffolk University as my safety school since I had read somewhere that it was primarily a night school for working professionals. To complete my list, I added UNC – Chapel Hill because I knew that it was a top tier school and I would only have to pay in-state tuition. I also added Duke because I figured if I got into Duke, I might be able to convince my wife to suck it up in North Carolina for three more years.

Yes, the process by which I chose my schools was really that superficial. Remember, this is one of those "learn from my mistakes" sections of the book. I spent no time actually researching the curriculum of the schools or their individual rankings. I did not peruse their websites. I did not talk to any alumni. I definitely did not even think about visiting the campuses. I essentially chose my schools based on geography and an idealized concept of what each school was about.

Next, I looked at their applications and realized that even though all of my schools had opened their admissions process way back in September, they were all still willing to take applications for another few weeks. I printed blank copies, stuffed them all in my backpack, and took them home that evening. Tucking myself into a corner of the couch with the dog at my feet and my wife watching Seinfeld, I began to fill out the paperwork with a ball point pen.

About half way through filling out the applications, I paused to wonder whether or not they would be more effective and persuasive if I dug out my old type writer. I rationalized to myself that the law school admissions committees were far more interested in the substantive meat of my applications then their presentation. They wanted to see my grades and my LSAT score and judge my ability to write, right? They could not possibly care whether or not I chose a pretty font or used heavy bond paper, could they?

Nowhere in this process did I stop to ask myself whether there was a better way. I signed my forms, wrote $600.00 in checks to cover the application fees, and sent off everything folded into business class envelopes and affixed with first class stamps.

Next on my list was the LSAT. Looking at the calendar, I saw there were two LSATs scheduled between the spring and the fall semester: one in February and one in June. I had just missed the February exam so I signed up for the June exam. I read on the LSAC website that the LSAT was not an exam you could truly study for, so I didn't do much to prepare other than make a note on the calendar hanging in our kitchen. The night before the exam, I went to bed early. I also made sure I had a few number two pencils. That was the extent of my preparations. As I learned later, although the exam is not really something for which you can study, it is something for which you can prepare. Unfortunately, my preparations were like preparing for a marathon by doing some toe-touching exercises the night before the race.

My applications had already been submitted. It was

early June. I did not get my LSAT score until sometime in the middle of the summer. I had not prepared, I had not studied, and I did about as well as you would expect.

Actually, to be completely honest, I did fine. Nothing outstanding but nothing terrible, either. I think that had more to do with the fact that there was only one games section on that exam (not that I knew what a games section was at the time) than the possibility that I was an excellent test taker. One thing was certain; I did not do nearly well enough to beat the LSAT average score for six of my ten potential schools.

Of course, by that point it was too late. I had already graduated from college and I was meandering through the summer working at the computer lab on campus. My LSAT score was a little low but it was too late to even consider applying to any other schools. It was only at this point that I bothered to begin reading the books, blogs, and forums on the web about law school applications. I read about preparing for the LSAT and how much weight it carries as compared to your GPA. I read about the value of a well-written essay and a well-presented application packet. I read about how important the financial aid process was to insuring you had the money to attend. In short, I read everything I should have read before I ever applied...and I slowly developed the horrible feeling that I had completely underestimated the law school application process.

Sure enough, the rejection letters began to arrive in mid July. Ultimately, I was rejected from nine of my ten schools. I was accepted by only one. The school I thought was the worst and the one I never really wanted to attend. I remember sitting on the couch and looking at the letters and thinking to myself,

'Where did I go wrong? I use to think I was a smart

guy. I used to think I was someone who was going to go out and do really important things. How did I end up here? Rejected by all but one of my schools...surely I am better than this.'

As I sat there, I thought about how I would do everything differently if only I had another chance. Then it dawned on me: I did have another chance. I was not committed to going to law school that fall. I could wait. There was nothing stopping me from throwing out the results of these applications and doing it all over again the *right* way next year.

That is exactly what I did. I learned the hard way, but I benefited from the experience. Giving myself the opportunity, as scary as it was, to resubmit my law school applications allowed me the opportunity to find the law school environment that was right for me. My knowledge of the law, my ability to advocate, even my self-esteem is better than it would have been had I settled for the one school to which I was accepted the first time. Now I get to share that experience with you and hopefully help you find the right school for you and maybe at the very least you will not waste six hundred bucks in application fees like I did.

Takeaway:

There is no right or wrong time to apply to law school, but you do need to make sure you approach the process well-versed in all the requirements. You only get one chance to make a first impression so give yourself as much time as you need to make it the best impression you can.

The Law School Application Calendar

As a general rule, law school applications become available sometime during the early fall of the year before the year you would like to attend. What this means is that you will be able to get the application in September of this year to start school in September of next year.

Even though the application is available in September, the school might not begin considering applications until a later date. All schools generally divide their application decision making process into at least two of the following three tranches:

1. Early Admission

This is a first-look early decision on individuals who submit a complete application by a specific date (usually sometime in September or early October). Early admission applicants generally get preferential consideration compared to everyone else. A few schools ask early admission applicants to commit to attending their school if they get accepted. In exchange, the early admission applicant gets early notification and can spend the rest of the year lording it over their fellow classmates and or co-workers. This informal contract goes by a variety of names but is generally referred to as "restricted early admission." Early admission, both open and restricted, is fading in popularity among law schools in favor of a rolling admissions process, but some schools have not yet changed, and you should check for early admission opportunities when you apply.

2. General Admission

This is the standard admissions process. Usually, it is a rolling process which means the school's applications committee meets every week to go over applications, rank them, and accept, deny, or defer on each application. General Admission usually opens at the same time that applications are made available and remains open until sometime in the middle of spring.

3. Waitlisted

This is the purgatory of the admissions process. The school's applications committee met, reviewed your application, and decided you were not good enough to accept and you were not bad enough to reject. They have waitlisted you instead. They will rank you on a list of an unknown quantity (meaning you could be number one or you could be number four hundred and one) and they will wait to see how many people turn down their acceptances. Then they will unceremoniously offer acceptances to the people on the ranked waitlist until they have filled up their incoming class. It is inglorious. It is insulting. I absolutely despise law school waitlists. When I was a 1L, the law school added and lost about a dozen people over the first few weeks of class due to the waitlist process. To me, it seems grossly unfair for a school to force someone to make such a life-altering decision with minimal notice and maximum pressure.

Should You Apply Early Admission?

The short answer is YES. You apply for early admission to every school on your list that offers unrestricted early admission consideration.

The slightly longer answer is that after you have made your dream list of appropriate schools (which we will discuss later in the chapter) then you will apply early admission to as many of them as you can. However, you will not select any restrictive early admission consideration (where you commit to attend if you are accepted) unless the school offering the restrictive early admission consideration is your unquestioned first choice.

No matter what, every application for the schools on your list will be completed and submitted as soon as the school will accept them—even if you are not submitting a particular application for early admission. There is no downside to getting your application into a school as soon as possible. If you plan your application calendar correctly, you will be able to time your submissions to coincide with the school's earliest window for consideration.

Important Dates to Write Down

Your ultimate goal is to have a complete application package submitted to the schools of your choice as soon as they will accept it. In addition to turning in the physical application (and application check), you will need to make sure your academic transcripts and recommendation letters are on file, your LSAT score has been reported, and that you have purchased all the CAS reports from the LSAC that you'll need for your applications. CAS reports, or Credential Assembly Service reports, is how the law schools to which you are applying see all your compiled data like transcripts and LSAT score. Do not worry. We discuss it in greater depth in Chapter Five.

So where do you begin?

Broadly speaking, you will want to begin the gathering of materials in the spring of the same year you apply. Another way of putting it is to say that you will begin the process eighteen months before your proposed start date at law school and you will actually submit your applications roughly twelve months before. Yet a third way of describing it is to say that if you wanted to attend Harvard in September of 2015, you would begin the application process in February of 2014 and you would submit the application in September of 2014. Does that make sense?

First Important Date:

When do you want to begin your studies?

The first date to write down is also one of the most important. When do you want to go to law school? This autumn? Next autumn? After you complete your undergraduate studies? After a master's or PhD degree? How about when your boyfriend plans to go to medical school? Or when your wife is planning on opening up her own accounting firm? The life plans of other family members are very important to consider. Law school is going to be an incredible challenge in the best of scenarios. Adding an unhappy or unsupportive spouse or partner to the equation is a recipe for disaster.

There is never one specific right time to apply to law school. Fortunately, the schools themselves make it a bit easier by only accepting students during the fall semester. You basically only have two choices: this fall...or the next one. My one piece of advice is to make sure you plan to give yourself enough time to apply and that you discuss this date with all the people who are going to be affected; spouse, children, long term significant others. The only thing harder than applying to law school is applying to law school but suddenly shifting gears and changing your application date. At best, it knocks you off balance. At worst, it wastes money and makes you look like a flake to the schools you most want to impress.

Second Important Date:

When are you taking the LSAT?

The LSAT is offered roughly four times a year: February, June, October, and December. Once your score is recorded, the LSAC will include it with all CAS reports for the next five years. If you take the LSAT more than once, all scores are reported along with the dates of the exams and any absences or cancellations.

How the schools choose to consider your LSAT score(s) is entirely up to them. Some schools take only the most recent exam score. Others average the scores. Still others take the highest of multiple scores. If the school is willing to disclose their methodology, you can usually find it by carefully perusing their admissions webpage or the LSAC website. The only thing you really need to know right now is that if you have an absolutely meltdown during the test, you really do not hurt yourself by taking it again.

For all these reasons and a few more that I will cover in Chapter Four, you should really sign up for the February LSAT exam date. The February date allows you plenty of time to prepare for the exam without the additional stress of undergraduate finals or the need to fill out application forms, write personal essays, and chase down recommendation letters.

While you are signing up for the LSAT, you should also give serious consideration to the potential value of a commercial preparatory course from a reputable vendor such as Kaplan or Princeton Review. While these courses are undeniably valuable to the applicants that use them simply because they provide a structured and systematic approach to preparing for and taking the LSAT, the extent of their value is questionable. None of the programs are cheap and some courses can cost several thousand dollars. An applicant also needs to be very wary of the many charlatans and fraudulent test prep companies on the internet that are just looking to make some quick cash.

In any case, if you are interested in a prep course, you should check the scheduling and sign up now. Kaplan offers courses that begin as late as two months from the date of the LSAT, but generally the longer you have to prepare for the exam, the better.

The February date also allows you plenty of time to sign up and prepare for the June exam date if you find out that you did poorly in February. Of course, that is not going to happen because you are reading this book. You are going to be so over-prepared for this exam that you will freak everyone else out due to your high degree of awesomeness.

Third Important Date:

When do you want to compile your recommendation letters and transcripts?

Academic transcripts are required for all institutions you have attended prior to applying to law school. This includes community college, vocational school, four year undergraduate programs, and any post-college degrees you have pursued. Similarly, most law schools require at least two recommendation letters from professors or employers who can speak to your ability, aptitude, and interest in the law. Both your transcripts and your recommendation letters will be submitted (either directly or by you) to the LSAC where they will be scanned and incorporated into your CAS Report.

Fortunately, there should not be a lot of debate about when you should submit these items to the LSAC. Because recommendation letters are notoriously difficult to acquire in a timely manner from professors, and because your old schools will be horribly slow in producing sealed and certified transcripts, you need to begin the process right after you finish the LSAT in February. You should aim to have everything in to the LSAC by the end of the summer. The last thing that should be sent to the LSAC should be your transcript covering any summer coursework or internships.

Fourth Important Date:

When are applications available from the schools to which you want to apply? When are each school's specific due dates? Where, in fact, do you want to apply?

The answer to these questions depend on the individual schools. At this point, you do not have a clear sense of where you want to apply yet. Sure, you may have one or two ideas and maybe a school that is an old family favorite, but you have no idea what your LSAT score is going to be like. You have no idea what financial aid packages are available. You have no idea where you will feel comfortable, welcome, and excited to learn.

Do not worry. All that comes later. For now, put together a big list of possibilities. Make it as broad as you want. My initial list when I finally decided to apply to law school the right way included over thirty law schools. Once you have assembled this list, carefully check their admissions websites and note when they will make their applications available for the next academic year. Also, take the opportunity to write down the following school-specific information:

— Early admission due date (if applicable)
— General Admission start and close date
— Financial Aid start and close date
— School Open House and applicant visit dates

If you get the opportunity, download the current year's and a couple of the previous years' applications. They will provide valuable insight into each school's application questions as well as an indication of where you will need to focus your personal essays. We will go into greater detail on the use of past applications in Chapter Eleven. For now, just try to find the last few years' applications for each school.

The Application Calendar Checklist

By now, you have developed some sort of calendar or timeline with all your important dates recorded. You will notice they cluster around the early fall and late spring. There is one more I want you to add. January 1. This is the first day for you to begin your federal financial aid forms.

It looks like a lot but you should not feel stressed. If you prepare like I show you, you will have all your materials put together weeks in advance. All you will need to do is tweak your answers and mail off your package as each application becomes available. Your name will be one of the first each admissions committee sees.

Take a moment to review the takeaways listed below. Use them as a check list to make sure you have covered all your bases. Next up: the LSAT!

Takeaway:

The law school application process, much like law school itself, is a marathon not a sprint. Give yourself plenty of time to prepare and present the best application package possible. As a general rule, you want to begin preparing to apply eighteen months prior to your date of attendance.

Takeaway:

Make a list of all the law schools you might be interested in. This is the time to dream big and be expansive. You will narrow your list down later. For now, keep your mind open to the potential for new experiences and new opportunities.

Takeaway:

Sign up for the February LSAT exam and decide if you want to utilize a commercial prep course.

Takeaway:

Plan to apply using early admission to as many schools as possible. Early admission is your friend. If early admission is not available, plan on sending your applications into the committees as soon as the rolling admissions process begins.

Takeaway:

Use your list of potential law schools to fill up your law school application calendar with all the important dates you will need to remember. You should have the LSAT exam date listed as well as when applications and financial aid packages are both available and due.

Takeaway:

Obtain the most recent application for each school in which you are interested. You will need them to prepare your application ahead of time.

The Generalized 10-Step Timeline of the Law School Application Process

This is a rough timeline of the application process from start to finish from the perspective of an undergraduate starting the third year of a four year degree. For those of you who left your undergraduate studies behind long ago, please adapt this checklist to your own personal circumstances.

01. Fall Semester, Junior Year—Realize you want to go to law school. Buy this book. Register for February LSAT and sign up for LSAT prep course (if applicable).

02. Beginning of Spring Semester, Junior Year— Take the LSAT exam. Create list of possible law schools.

03. Middle of Spring Semester, Junior Year— Receive score for the LSAT exam. Weep or celebrate as necessary.

04. End of Spring Semester, Junior Year—submit transcripts with GPA to LSAC. Finalize list of law schools. Begin asking for recommendations. Begin visiting schools.

05. Summer Time—Continue asking for recommendations. Continue visiting schools. Prepare personal questions and essay responses based on old applications.

06. Beginning of Fall Semester, Senior Year— Applications and Financial Aid forms become available. Fill out and submit. You are still visiting schools.

07. Middle of Fall Semester, Senior Year—All applications and financial aid forms are completely submitted.

08. End of Fall Semester, Senior Year—Receive notice from schools with early admission. Weep or celebrate as necessary.

09.   Beginning of Spring Semester, Senior Year—Complete taxes. Submit Federal Financial Aid Forms. Amend all individual law school financial aid applications with required information. Cross fingers and maybe go skiing.

10.   End of Spring Semester, Senior Year—Receive all acceptance/rejection letters and financial aid packages. Graduate from college (Congrats!). Make law school choice. Submit final transcripts.

10b.   Have a great summer! Get ready to go to law school.

CHAPTER FOUR
TACKLING THE LAW SCHOOL ADMISSIONS TEST

THE LAW SCHOOL Admissions Test, better known as the LSAT, is the massive brick wall that all law school applicants must scale. Rich or poor, smart or dumb—everyone has to take the LSAT. You will either climb over it or crash into it, but one way or the other you will deal with it. However, I promise if you read this chapter, I will do my best to provide you with a proverbial grappling hook and a set of crampons so that you have the very best chance at conquering this obstacle from the very beginning.

What the LSAT Means to Your Application

How to value your LSAT score is completely up to the individual schools. That information is usually available somewhere on the admissions sections of their websites. Go check it out for each school to which you are interested in applying. I have no doubt it will make for some interesting reading.

Now, let me tell you the reality: the LSAT is weighted more than your GPA, more than your personal essays, and a boatload more than your recommendations. I am not sure there is an admissions professional out there who will be completely honest about their process, but I willing to bet my eyeteeth that there is not a single student at Harvard who scored a 140 on their LSAT but still got into Harvard Law School on the basis of their 4.0 undergraduate GPA and glowing recommendations.

What does this mean to you? This exam is *very* important. Treat it like a wild mustang. If you do things right, this beast will take you places like you are strapped to a rocket. If you do things wrong, it will throw you on the ground and step on your head.

The Nuts and Bolts of the LSAT

The LSAT is a multiple choice exam lasting roughly four hours. In my personal experience (I took it twice), the total time from when you arrive at the testing center to when you leave is roughly six to seven hours. Make sure you are well-rested, well-watered and well-fed, and that you have used the bathroom. In fact, treat it like you would prepare for a marathon and you will be fine.

The exam itself is divided into six 35-minute timed sections including one ungraded experimental section and one writing sample. The writing sample is sent, untouched, to every school requesting your LSAT score. The other five sections are multiple choice and divided into three categories: Reading Comprehension, Logical Reasoning, and Analytical Reasoning (aka: Games). The experimental section will be masked to look like one of the other four sections. The LSAC folks say that you will not know, but I am pretty sure I was able to tell both times I took the exam. The first time because there was an extraordinarily easy section in the middle of my exam and the second time because there was an extra Analytical Reasoning section so difficult that I only managed to answer one set of questions before my time was up.

Very briefly, here is what I remember about each section:

Reading Comprehension

The Reading Comprehension section is exactly what it sounds like. You read...and comprehend. It is just like the SATs except several levels harder. Generally, you will be given four writing samples. Each sample will be roughly 700-1500 words long and contain several complex concepts or ideas. You will read each sample carefully and then answer five to ten highly nuanced multiple choice questions about the ideas expressed. If you are not a good reader or if you are not prepared, this will drive you crazy. The first time I took the exam, I was able to eliminate one or two of the answers for each question as being obviously incorrect. I then spent the rest of my time slowly going nuts as I moved between the three or four remaining answers trying to figure out which one was *most* correct. I was, as a former professor of mine use to say, "...frozen by the enormity of the decision before me." Whatever you want to call it, I was stuck.

Logical Reasoning

I think of this as Reading Comprehension Lite. Logical Reasoning is the word problem portion of the exam and, in my humble opinion, the easiest part. Do not think I am saying that it is particularly easy. It is just easier than Reading Comprehension or Games. In a nutshell, you will receive a short statement and then be asked one or two questions about it. You will need to be able to process the logical or illogical concept within the statement and answer the questions based on your understanding. Does that make sense? Do not stress too much. If you google the phrase "LSAT Sample Logical Reasoning Questions," you will find tons of examples. They are challenging, but not as bad as the next section.

Analytical Reasoning

This is the dreaded "Games" section. Actually, it is not really fair for me to call it 'dreaded.' Some people really like this section. You know—crazy people. The kind of people who really like the Rubik's Cube and don't think Tetris gets fun until the fiftieth level. However, if you are asking me, I will tell you that I think the Games section is as close as we, as a society, can come to voluntary mental torture.

Remember the old word puzzles your middle school math teacher would put at the end a test? The type of puzzle that would look something like this:

'Five cars are parked in five different parking spaces. The five spaces are labeled A, B, C, D, and E. The five cars have five different license plates labeled 1, 2, 3, 4, and 5. Car 1 is parked in E. Car 5 is parked in A. Car 4 always arrives after Car 2 and Car 3 never takes space C. If Car 2 parks in B, where does Car 4 park?'

Now, the Games section is just like that except the question is:

'If Car 2 parks in B, what color is Car 4?'

I know. It makes my brain hurt just thinking about it again. Of course, I am exaggerating a little bit. I promise you will have all the data in front of you necessary to solve the problem. You might just need to be extremely careful in how you parse out that data.

Takeaway:

The LSAT is a bastard of exam. Fortunately, you can prepare for it.

Is a Commercial Prep Course Worth It?

This is a tough question to answer. The short answer is it depends on if you can afford it. Prep courses can be very expensive. On the one hand, the feedback is not entirely clear that every individual (or even most individuals) show a substantial improvement in their test scores. On the other hand, most people who take a prep course at least go into the LSAT on exam day with a much higher sense of self-confidence. They also get the experience of having taken the test under similar conditions multiple times. That is certainly helpful in many intangible and immeasurable ways.

As of the time of this writing, the Kaplan "Extreme" Prep Course costs just over $1500 to prepare you for the upcoming February LSAT. Judging from their website, it looks like a fairly intensive program lasting three months (three times per week) and they provide a complete library of previously used LSAT questions. Does that make it worth it? I think that is a decision each person needs to make for themselves, but here is my personal decision-making tree for the LSAT prep courses.

How to Decide if You Should Take a LSAT Prep Course

1. Get a practice test book. Sit down and recreate the testing conditions to the best of your ability. Close yourself off at a desk in your apartment or go to the library if you need to. Take the test. Be very firm with yourself on the time limits. DO NOT CHEAT.
2. Grade the test. Take your score and subtract 5 points.
3. Look at your list of dream schools. What is your number one choice? Go to either the school's website or the current U.S. News ranking list. Look at the LSAT average.
4. Compare your score to the school's average. Is your score in the top half or higher?
5. If yes, then you are already there. I do not think you need to take a prep course. You should study on your own and try to prepare yourself to have a good test day.
6. If no, then I think you might (and I stress *might*) benefit from a prep course. Take a look at what is out there? Do you see anything appealing? Can you afford any of them? If so, then sign up and good luck.

Takeaway:

If you can afford it and you need a higher score than you are getting on your own, a commercial prep course just might be worth it.

The Ugly Truth about the LSAT

I am not going to tell you any secret strategies to beat the LSAT because there are not any secret strategies to tell. The LSAC folks are actually pretty up front and honest on their website and in their literature: the LSAT is not a test for which you can really study.

It has been my experience (and the experience of a great number of friends and colleagues) that the score you get on the practice tests is roughly five points higher than the score you get on the actual LSAT. If you take the exam multiple times, your score will likely vary inside a fairly tight six point window. Meaning if you score a 150, you are likely to consistently score between a 147 and a 153 if you were to take the exam over and over again.

While a prep course can provide you with experience in taking the exam under similar physical conditions and can also expose you to the types of questions you will see, in my opinion it is extremely unlikely that a prep course can improve your score more than a couple of points. Is that worth the money? Only you can decide for yourself.

The first time I took the LSAT, I scored in the 86th percentile and that was without doing one shred of preparation. It was a good score but not one that was going to get me into Harvard. The second time I took the LSAT, I prepared on my own for two months. I did multiple practice sections. I read everything I could get my hands on about taking the test. I also bought a book of old exams and tested myself every Sunday until the weekend of the exam. For all that preparation, my score went up one point.

Think about that.

No effort = X

With effort = X+1

Would I have benefited from taking an organized prep course? Intellectually, I can repeat what I have written before and say it is highly unlikely...but in my heart, I kind of wish I could go back in time and take a prep course anyway. Who knows? I felt pretty confident walking into the exam both times that I took it, but I've always had a little shadow of doubt in my mind that I would have been even better off if I had taken a structured prep course.

Should I Take the LSAT More than Once?

I debated combining this question with the previous bit we just covered. Like I said before, the vast majority of test takers in the vast majority of situations will not benefit from retaking the exam. However, there are a few situations where re-taking the exam might be beneficial.

1. Your official score is radically lower than the average score of your practice exams.
2. You became sick, you had an equipment failure, or there was an otherwise unavoidable event that interrupted or disrupted your ability to take your exam.
3. You failed to score high enough to make yourself competitive and you know in your gut you can do better than you did.

In these three limited situations, I would recommend you sign up for the exam again. I would also recommend you seriously consider taking a commercial prep course to help guide your preparations this time.

What if I failed to do as well as I needed to get into Harvard, Yale, Stanford etc...should I retake the LSAT and hope I have a miracle performance?

Life is often times hard and unfair. We should all take a moment to reflect on how lucky we are to be exactly where we are right now. I know I am lucky because I am living in a society where I had the opportunity to go to law school (even though I am pretty sure there is a federal lien on my vital organs in the event that I die young) and write a book about my experiences.

I am pretty sure you are lucky because you live in a society where you are able to contemplate going to law school and can even afford to buy a book about the process.

Are we all feeling fairly grateful for our lots in life? Good, because here comes the hard truth:

You will not go to Harvard, Yale, Stanford etc. Sorry. Those schools might be for other people but they will not be for you.

It hurts. I know. The day I realized that I was not going to be competitive for Harvard was the day I knew without a doubt that my parents were kind-hearted liars. There actually are things in life I am not going to achieve no matter how hard I set my mind to them.

That said, I will go into greater detail later on about why it doesn't matter. For now, just accept that you are going to need to grow up a little bit and modify your dreams. Taking the LSAT again would just be a waste of time. You would be tilting at windmills with a small chance of success and a large chance of damaging your current position.

> ## Takeaway:
>
> For 99% of the people, 99% of the time, there is no benefit to taking the LSAT more than once. Your job, therefore, is to make your one attempt the very best it can possibly be.

CHAPTER FIVE
INTERPRETING YOUR LSAT SCORE

It is late February or early March. Winter squats over everything like an unwelcome guest. Some schools call this time period 'The Doldroms,' other schools call it 'The Dark Ages.' If you are in Florida, you are enjoying reasonably awesome days in the high sixties and low seventies. If you are in Maine, you are wading through four feet of snow and cursing those bastards living in Florida. If you are in southern California, you are watching all of this with bemused interest and wondering if snow is worse than earthquakes. However, the one thing you all have in common is that you have just received your LSAT score.

Although I know that every single person reading this book will ignore this advice, I am still going to say it: Do not open the letter/e-mail/fax/website right away. Wait until later when you are someplace quiet and alone.

Regardless of whether or not it is great news or horrible news, you are going to need some time to digest it and figure out what it means.

Are you ready?

Are you really ready? Really, *really* ready?

Okay. We all have our fingers crossed for you. Go ahead and check the score. We will be waiting right here when you get done.

Understanding Your LSAT Score, aka: At What Point Do I Worry?

So, you could not do worse than 120 or better than 180. Where did you fall on this spectrum? The scaled average is usually placed right at 151. The lower the score below this statistical mid-point, the more difficult you will find it to gain admittance into a law school. While it is not impossible, it is extremely difficult.

Here is my rough assessment of what LSAT scores mean. By the way, this is my personal assessment based on personal experience and observation. The LSAC might say something different and I can almost guarantee every law school admissions office is going to soften their language to avoid committing to any particular bright-line standard, but this is what I think no one is willing to say:

120-139—Completely unacceptable. I wish I could sugarcoat it, but I can't. You must take the LSAT again or think about a different career path. The only schools that seriously consider scores in this range are the sort of schools you should never seriously consider (with apologies to Groucho Marx).

140-149—This is not a good score range but depending on where you want to go, you might be able to work with it. You will see some Tier 4 schools with LSAT averages in this range.

150-159—This is the range with the most variability. Some of your Tier 2 and most of your Tier 3 and Tier 4 schools have classes which dominate in this scoring range. To breathe easy, though, you really want a 155-159.

160-169—Now you are cooking with fire! These are the 85th to 90th percentile scores. You should be fine with most Tier 2 and some Tier 1 schools.

170-180—These are 90th to 99th percentile scores. You can give the top twenty-five schools a serious look. Congratulations. You are a brainiac.

How did you do? The higher you scored, the more relaxed you are feeling, right?

Not really. I know. My guess is that is because you are most likely already in love.

Tell me I am wrong. Go ahead, tell me that at this point, you have not already begun fantasizing about your dream school. Maybe you fell in love with Harvard after watching *The Paper Chase* or *Love Story*—just please do not let it be *Legally Blonde*. Maybe you visited our nation's capital and now have your heart set on Georgetown University. Maybe you interned with Green Peace this summer and can only see yourself fulfilling your life's purpose at the number one environmental law school in the country: Vermont Law School.

Author's Note:

You should infer absolutely no sense of bias simply because your author attended Vermont Law School and can definitively state that it is the best law school in the country.

No matter which school it is that has captured your heart and imagination, I think I have stressed enough by now that the LSAT score is the predominant gate keeper, so go take a look at the school's 25/75 spread. No doubt if you scored inside it, you are happy right now. If you did not, you are crushed.

The Sin of Academic Lust

You should not be, though. You only *think* you are in love. I am telling you right now that this is not love. This is infatuation. This is academic lust. This is definitely NOT love and you should not let yourself think of it as love (or destiny, or a perfect fit, or any other emotionally charged descriptive synonym).

You do not want to be in love with the schools to which you are applying (at least not yet) because people in love do stupid things. They take blind leaps of faith. They sacrifice what is in their best interests. They agree to assume stupefying amounts of student loan debt in exchange for the right to wear a particular school's sweatshirt. I hope you realize that this is, of course, absolutely insane.

Think of me as your best friend at a bar. I am your wingman. I am your friend who promised to make sure you did not do anything stupid at the club. Well, I am here to tell you that your moment of stupidity is right now. It is not six months from now when you actually send in your acceptance response card and deposit check. It is right now. This is when the romance starts. This is when you begin to buy into the seductive brochures, the promising statistics about job placement, and the great photos of campus life.

Do not worry. You are not alone. I am here with you. I am tugging on your sleeve. I am whispering in your ear to please notice that the school you are eyeballing from across the dance floor is wearing a wedding ring or looks like it might have Chlamydia.

You do not want those schools. You may not know what school you do want, but you do know that you want to be smart about the whole process. You want to be analytical about it. You want to be stone cold ruthless about it. Why? Because ten years from now that school is not going to remember your name except once a year when it calls to ask you for more money. Meanwhile, you will still be sending off those student loan checks every month with no end in sight.

Here is the reality: In law school, if not necessarily any other place in life, it is better to be the big fish in the little pond than the little fish struggling mightily to swim in the ocean. It is better to be the full-ride scholarship student graduating debt-free with a 3.9 GPA from a Tier Four public school *where you are happy* than some poor bastard struggling in the bottom ten percent of the class at Harvard and buried under $150,000 in student loans.

Q: Do you know what the valedictorian of Yale Law School and the lowest ranked graduate of North Carolina Central University School of Law have in common?

A: They are both lawyers.

Happiness is underrated when talking about applying to law school. The assumption is that if you get into the highest ranked school that you can possibly get into, you will be, as a matter of logic, happy.

This is complete horse crap.

If you take the time to do your research and to compare your choices in an analytical and dispassionate manner, you stand a much better chance of attending a school that is a great fit for you academically, socially, and financially, and—as a matter of logic—you do have a much higher chance of being happy.

We are going to talk about finding the right school for you a little later on. In this particular metaphor, there are over two hundred fish in the sea but only a handful are going to be good fish for you. For now, we need to first figure out who the 'you' is. We need to take stock of the attributes you bring to the law school application package.

Takeaway:

The LSAT does not define who you are, but it does give you a ceiling on where you are likely to be successful when applying. It is important to remember, however, that the highest ranked school on your list is *no more likely* to guarantee your personal happiness and success in life than the lowest ranked school. Do not fall for academic lust.

CHAPTER SIX
WHAT YOU BRING TO THE TABLE

S O WHAT ARE the variables that law schools are looking at on your application? You can break them into five major areas:

1. Biographical Data
2. Previous Academic Record
3. LSAT Score
4. Recommendations
5. Personal Questions and Essays

Each one of these areas provides an opportunity for you to present a snapshot of yourself to the admissions committees. More importantly, they are also an opportunity for you to compare your personal needs and desires to what each law school has to offer. If you are an experiential learner who develops best through practice and practical applications, you will not benefit from an old-school Socratic methodology. If you are a researcher at heart who lives for the library and the solid reliability of references and footnotes, then a law school's extensive development of Semester-in-Practice internships will not really mean a lot to you. What you are looking for from your law school experience is just as important as what the law schools are looking for from you. Do not discount your needs.

Let me take a moment to define how each section impacts and enhances your ability to present yourself. Do not worry—we will get into the nitty-gritty of how best to prepare each section when we discuss the application process in Chapter Eleven.

1. Biographical Data

Diversity is rarely discussed directly in relation to the consideration of individual application packages, but the fact is that it is in the best interests of a law school to have a class of students representing the broadest possible spectrum of society. The diversity of the student body informs class discussions and enhances debate. Remember that the concept of diversity is not limited strictly to designations of gender and race. Are you the first person in your family to go to college? Was your mother or father in the military so you grew up almost entirely overseas? Are you a Hasidic Jew applying to a Catholic law school? All these are examples of an opportunity to highlight how your unique background can contribute to the diversity of the law school.

2. Previous Academic Record

Your college transcripts are, for better or for worse, your résumé in the law school application package. A candidate's GPA is second only to the LSAT score in consideration of how much weight it carries. Unfortunately, you will have a tough time changing your GPA if you are not currently happy with it. I will show you one possible method in Chapter Eleven for those applicants who absolutely must improve their GPA but for everyone else: consider it a marker that divides the schools for which you are competitive from the schools for which you are not.

3. LSAT Score

I think we pummeled this topic pretty thoroughly in Chapter Five. Your LSAT score, like your GPA, is a marker that gives you an indication of where you are competitive and where you are not. If you absolutely must change your LSAT score, you will need to take the exam again. Just be warned, as I wrote previously, that it is very difficult to make a substantial change in your LSAT score.

4. Recommendations

Every law school will require between one and three recommendation letters written by professors or employers who can comment on your qualities (both academic and otherwise) and your ability to be a successful law student. Compared to your GPA and your LSAT score, recommendation letters do not carry a tremendous amount of weight, but they are the only part of the application where *somebody else* has the opportunity to tell the school how awesome you are.

5. Personal Questions and Essays

Less important than the LSAT and GPA but more important than the recommendations, the personal questions and essay questions in each application are an opportunity for you to present your story in the most appealing and beneficial light. This is you selling yourself.

Making Your List Manageable

We are now going to begin the process of massaging your huge list of possible law schools into a much more manageable list of a dozen or so top contenders. Think of this process like the first few episodes of American Idol. You have done the open casting call. Any school with a pulse that looked even slightly interesting got thrown on the list. Now you are going to start brutally hacking and slashing your way down to the final contestants – the ones you are going to structure the whole application season around.

They say that the first cut is always the deepest so let's take your LSAT score. Assuming you have made the decision to keep your score, you can now narrow your list by removing those schools that need a higher LSAT score than you have to offer. Most schools report an LSAT score range from bottom 25 percent to top 75 percent. If your score does not meet the bottom 25 percent, go ahead and drop that school from your list. It stinks. I know and I am sorry, but you are not competitive. Applying would be a waste of your time and money.

Now, take a deep breath because we are going to do the same thing with your GPA. If you have already finished your previous academic career, then you have a finalized set of figures from which to work. If you are still in school, give yourself a rough estimate of how your final semester will shake out. Although you will send your current transcript to the LSAC for inclusion into the CAS reports, you will also need to provide a final transcript reflecting your complete GPA. Similar to your LSAT score, average GPAs for each school are reported on a range from 25 percent to 75 percent. While it is less common than with LSAT scores, you should still check to see if your GPA precludes you from any of the schools on your list.

Personal Experience

I went to two undergraduate institutions with a multi-year break in between so I needed to report both sets of transcripts. Although some schools accepted the GPA from my degree-granting institution (a comfortable 3.6), other schools combined that score with the GPA from my original undergraduate institution (where my GPA was a cringe-inducing 2.2). The painful result was that I wasted time, money, and hope on some schools where I should have known my combined GPA of 2.7 was going to knock me out of competition for admission.

Please note that I have not advised you to remove any of the schools for which your LSAT score or GPA exceeds the 75 percent range. These schools are your go-to schools. You are going to be much more discerning in removing these schools from your list. After all, they really want your LSAT and GPA numbers for their U.S. News rankings and many will be willing to offer you a substantial financial aid package to get you to join their student bodies. If there is one thing I will repeat throughout this book, it is the fact that the cheaper you can obtain an appropriately fulfilling and enriching law school education, the better.

Takeaway:

Now that you have your LSAT score and your GPA, drop the schools that want numbers higher than you have. Keep the schools that want numbers lower than you have. The first group will not accept you but the second group just might be willing to throw massive scholarships at you.

Halfway There

What does your list look like now? By this point you have stripped out the schools whose hard statistical data puts them out of your league. The schools remaining on your list are all schools that you are—at a minimum—competitive for acceptance. If you created your list correctly, these are all schools in which you also have at least a passing interest.

It gets a little harder from here. Your goal is to take your list and strip it down even further until you are left with a core group of six to eight law schools. Some people may be comfortable with as few as three and others may want to have as many as twelve. From my personal experience, I can tell you that I kept six schools on my short list of possible applicants the second time around.

How do you trim your list down to the core possibilities? That is entirely up to you. There are a variety of different factors, some tangible and some intangible, that could have a dramatic influence on your time in law school. A successful experience is not just about the academic rigor and job placement programs that a particular school offers, it is also about where you feel comfortable, happy, and capable of learning. A happy student is a good student and an unhappy student is definitely not.

For example, you might want to look at geography as a possible factor. The University of Hawaii might look beautiful, but how likely are you to be happy there if your parents are your best friends and they retired to northern Maine? You could also consider the school's environment. If you love big urban city centers, do you think you will be fulfilled with the rustic pleasures of the University of Iowa? Looking at the other side of that coin: if you love the rural life, do you think riding the subway to Columbia University every morning is going to be tolerable?

You might also consider school culture. For me, I kept Campbell University Law School in North Carolina on my list of possible law schools for a long time because of its location and the possibility of significant financial aid. I finally decided that the school's overt religious message was too strong for me. For others, it might be exactly what they are looking for, but it was the opposite of the secular environment I was seeking. I knew that even if I received a substantial scholarship, I would likely be unhappy at Campbell and I decided to remove it from my list.

Ultimately, you will need to decide what factors are important to you. The goal is get your list down to something with which you can work. Remember that nothing is written in stone. If you have finished your list and you really want to add back a school that you previously cut because it is beyond the reach of your LSAT score, go ahead and do it. Stranger things have happened and you might get lucky. It is your list. You own it.

Take your time to mull it all over. Add and subtract as you consider the things that are important to you. Make sure you get your transcripts submitted to the LSAC at the end of the semester. If you want, skip to Chapter Ten and read the section on recommendations. You can get started on those if you have the opportunity. Other than that, take the rest of the semester to research law schools and consider your choices. In the next chapter, we will discuss ranking and visiting your candidates.

Takeaway:

Combine your variable data with your personal goals to begin winnowing down your list of prospective schools. The schools you apply to should meet your admissions standards just as much as you need to meet theirs.

CHAPTER SEVEN
VISITING SCHOOLS: THE GOOD, THE BAD, AND THE UGLY

W OW. TIME IS really starting to fly. At this point, you have taken the LSAT and gathered together your academic transcripts. As you conclude the spring semester at your current institution, make sure you get the updated transcripts into the LSAC. You have also surveyed the whole wide world of law schools and narrowed the possibilities down to a group of schools for which you are a competitive candidate. You have since further narrowed that group of schools into a relatively small collection of handpicked candidates which you think might be competitive candidates for you.

From this point onward, the timeline for applying begins to truncate. Although we separate the discussion of visiting law schools from the discussion on applying, you will not necessarily experience them separately. Depending on your personal schedule, you may find yourself visiting schools after you have already submitted your application. Remember the 10-Step Timeline for Law School Applications from

Chapter Three? I have reprinted it below. Remember: the process is unique to each applicant, so all I can really tell you is that your personal experience should follow roughly the following progression:

01.   Fall Semester, Junior Year—Realize you want to go to law school. Buy this book. Register for February LSAT and sign up for LSAT prep course (if applicable).

02.   Beginning of Spring Semester, Junior Year— Take the LSAT exam. Create list of possible law schools.

03.   Middle of Spring Semester, Junior Year— Receive score for the LSAT exam. Weep or celebrate as necessary.

04.   End of Spring Semester, Junior Year—submit transcripts with GPA to LSAC. Finalize list of law schools. Begin asking for recommendations. Begin visiting schools.

05.   Summer Time—Continue asking for recommendations. Continue visiting schools. Prepare personal questions and essay responses based on old applications.

06.   Beginning of Fall Semester, Senior Year— Applications and financial aid forms become available. Fill out and submit. You are still visiting schools.

07.   Middle of Fall Semester, Senior Year—All applications and financial aid forms are completely submitted.

08.   End of Fall Semester, Senior Year—Receive notice regarding Early Admission. Weep or celebrate as necessary.

09.   Beginning of Spring Semester, Senior Year— Complete taxes. Submit Federal Financial Aid Forms. Amend all individual law school financial aid applications with required information. Cross fingers and maybe go skiing.

10.   End of Spring Semester, Senior Year—Receive all acceptance/rejection letters and financial aid packages. Graduate from college (Congrats!). Make law school choice. Submit final transcripts.

10b. Have a great summer!—Get ready to go to law school.

If you can keep this general timeline in mind, you will be fine moving through the process. For now, enjoy this brief lull in the action since it will get much busier towards the end of the summer. In fact, now would be the perfect time to begin your process of shopping for your perfect school.

Remember that the law school application process should be just as much about the school auditioning itself to you as it is about you applying to the school. Finding that perfect fit should be a slow and methodical process involving as many campus visits, classroom observations, and meetings with students, professors, admissions officials, and financial aid offices as you can possibly fit into your schedule.

Types of School Visits

There are a couple of different ways you can visit a potential law school. You can be invited to an open house where all the applicants are given a tour of the campus. You can request an individual tour. You can even just show up one day and see how the school's admissions office handles surprise visitors. But wait. Before you head out to conduct a surprise inspection of Harvard, let's examine the pros and cons of each type of visit.

1. The Open House

Think of this as the law school's party. The floor is clean, the food is fresh, and everyone is wearing their nicest clothes. The Open House is the law school's commercial for itself. Make sure you get invited to the party by registering with the law school's admissions office (usually right on the admissions office's webpage).

Positives

The Open House is a controlled event. Usually there is a schedule of events and the law school brings out its big guns. You will have someone senior in the school's administration speak to the guests as well as one or two of the big name faculty. More importantly, you will hear from the folks in the admissions office and possibly even get some face time. The real benefit of the Open House is that you will see a good general overview of that particular school's culture and what the administration thinks is important for you to see.

Negatives

Like I wrote above, the Open House is a controlled event. It is controlled by the law school. You will see what they want you to see, hear what they want you to hear, and experience exactly the environment that they want you to experience. Think of the Open House as a scene from the Jim Carrey movie *The Truman Show* and you will kind of get the right idea. The faculty members that attend will be handpicked for their prestige and their ability to impress potential students. The students that participate will be carefully selected by the school to make sure they represent only the most positive aspects of student life. Even the campus tour, if there is one, will be carefully choreographed to take you through the best parts of campus while avoiding the areas that look less than ideal.

Personal Experience

I went to an open house at a law school in New England when I was applying the second time around. I was favorably disposed to this law school because of its position in the U.S. News rankings, the prestige of the larger university system to which it belonged, and its location in the New England area. I thought the brochure looked great and I had read very favorable statistics regarding new graduate job placement. In short, I was eager to like this school.

The Open House was nice enough. A group of prospective students including myself were ushered into a room in the main administrative building. Somebody from admissions spoke briefly about the school's history and a faculty member waxed poetic about an overseas trip he had taken with a handful of third year students to study some obscure aspect of some obscure field of international law. I don't want to say that I was bored, but I will say that I was waiting to hear about aspects of the law school that were slightly more relevant to a potentially new student like me.

There was a brief question and answer period afterwards, but specific questions about financial aid were deftly referred back to the financial aid office— which had incidentally failed to provide anyone to talk to us. Since those sorts of questions made up the bulk of our queries, the whole Q&A section did not last very long. We asked a few courtesy questions about course loads and somebody asked the professor if he taught any first-year classes (he did not). Other than that, we all stood around and waited for something else to happen.

Finally, a couple of third year law students showed up and took us for a tour of campus. One student seemed only capable of discussing his experiences in law school as they related to his support of the university's football team. He was very proud of the fact that he had attended the same university as an undergraduate which apparently meant he had managed to get preferred student seating at the games for seven consecutive years. As far as he was concerned, as long as the football team rocked, the law school rocked. The other student told us that she was a dual degree student and had actually finished all of her law school coursework the semester before. She was going to spend the final semester of school finishing off her MBA degree. She was more than happy to talk about the law firm that had already made her an offer the summer before, but did not seem to have anything substantive to say about her law school experience. Don't get me wrong. I am not intending to describe this student as vapid, self-centered, or uninterested in our concerns. It is just that I have no doubt that her first year of law school was a distant memory; sepia-toned with nostalgia and half-obscured by the blinding light from her bright and lucrative future as an associate at a Big Law firm.

Overall, the Open House left me feeling disappointed. This was a school I had been really excited about and I wanted to believe that it felt the same way about me. Instead, I had the sense that the school had held its Open House because it had to, because not holding one would have seemed strange. I had the sense that the administration felt the law school was too important to bother stooping so low as to "sell" itself to prospective students, and I drove back home acutely aware that I still knew very little about that law school and whether or not I would be a good fit. Unfortunately, because that was my only opportunity to make it up to New England before making my decision, I never had a chance to revisit that particular law school to see if my first impression had been wrong.

2. The Drop-In

Think of this as the exact opposite of the Open House. The idea is that you just show up one day at the law school and you see what happens. I will tell you up front that if you choose to try this, you need to be really careful how you go about it or else you will be perceived as being clueless or rude. My recommendation is to call the admissions office of the law school either the night before or the morning of the day you want to stop by. Tell them you found yourself with a sudden opportunity to visit that you would not have otherwise had. I recommend you use something along the lines of,

"I happen to be in your city for a conference and this is my only chance to come by,"

or,

"My classes were cancelled today due to a water leak at my university, and I have the whole morning off."

Sometimes admissions offices will try to accommodate your requests completely. Sometimes they will tell you they only do organized events. Sometimes they will offer you a brochure and a self-guided tour. Regardless, be respectful of the answer they give you. The last thing you want is for your name to be associated with the adjective "annoying."

Positives

You have the chance to see what daily life is really like at the law school. All the little things that make up a day in the life of a law student, from parking and public transportation options to construction near the campus and options for grabbing lunch in the middle of the school day. If you are lucky, the school might allow you the opportunity to observe a class or catch five minutes with the head of admissions or financial aid. These are golden opportunities that make the Drop-In a valuable method for evaluating law schools on the fly.

Negatives

You run the risk of seeing nothing. The school might be closed for some reason or the admissions office might be doing an off-site meeting. There is still plenty you can see, but if you needed to travel a long distance to get to the school, then you could find yourself feeling like the trip was not quite worth it. You could also run the risk of getting in trouble with the campus police if you start wandering around uninvited and unaccompanied. As I mentioned above, you do not want the law school thinking you are annoying or irritating. Sure, you want to catch them a little off guard so you can see the real school and not just the sugar coated vision presented during Open Houses, but you do not want the law school to decide that you are not worth the trouble.

Personal Experience

I did a Drop-In at Georgetown University one early fall day. I happened to be in DC during the week to visit my sister who lived in the Maryland suburbs. I called Georgetown in the morning. The person who answered the phone for the admissions office was very nice but informed me that there was no one available that day to see me. Oh well. It was a fair response to my request. That is the risk you run when you try a Drop-In.

A quick check of Georgetown's website shows that Georgetown currently offers a variety of options for the visiting applicant. You can take a guided tour or observe a first year class. You just need to conform to Georgetown's scheduled offerings. Make sure you RSVP as well. I think it is safe to assume from this that drop-in visits remain discouraged.

I rode the metro down to campus as I imagined I would if I was renting an apartment in the area. Following my map, I realized the law school's buildings are not actually in Georgetown but rather located over by Union Station. I also learned that the rush hour traffic on both the metro and the streets was absolutely crazy. There was not a single quiet place in the area for someone to get away from the noise except at the law school's library. Watching the number of people moving in and out of the buildings, I could imagine how packed they must be. I felt closed in and claustrophobic just watching everyone.

It may sound silly, but I had a vision of Georgetown that involved *actually living in Georgetown*. I wanted to study on a campus that overlooked the Potomac and exuded a sense of quiet solemnity and academic seriousness. That vision was shattered by the reality of a law school centered squarely in the downtown bustle of Washington, D.C. I just could not reconcile the reality with my ideal daydream.

Would it have kept me from attending Georgetown University Law School if say, the school had offered me a full scholarship? No, probably not. But I think I can safely say that my interest in Georgetown as a top contender on my short list was significantly reduced. If I had not already submitted my application, I probably would have picked a different school upon which to spend the application fee. The urban setting and the reality of fighting the traffic every day was a real turn off for me.

3. The Scheduled Visit

This is the classic method of visiting a law school and the one I prefer the most. All you do is call the law school's admissions office and tell them that you will be in the area at some point in the future (you pick the time) and would like to stop by and visit the school. Be sure to tell them that you would like to meet with someone in the admissions office and the financial aid office if possible. Again, like in the case of the Drop-In, you will need to respect whatever answer the law school gives you. Unlike in the case of the Drop-In, you are fully entitled to think it strange if the law school is unwilling or incapable of supporting a request for a scheduled visit.

Positives

The Scheduled Visit gives you one-on-one time with both the admissions office and with the financial aid office. Think of it as an informal interview for both you and them. If the meeting goes well, you will be remembered as the nice applicant who liked the school enough to pay a visit. It is a small advantage but it will pay dividends. Studies show that being able to put a face to a name increases the ability to recall information about a person. Believe me, if the decision on financial aid comes down to deciding between you and another applicant, it cannot hurt that the head of the financial aid office met you and has a good opinion of you.

In addition, you will have the opportunity to see the campus and to focus on the areas that matter most to you. You also might be able to sit in a class and observe real students asking real questions. You get the benefits of the Drop-In while minimizing the risk.

Negatives

There is still always the chance that the law school will try to put on a show, but I think it is far less likely. Still unlikely but more plausible is that the admissions office will simply choose to deny your request. In those cases, you should really ask yourself if that particular school is a place you want to spend the next three years of your life. What would happen if you had a personal problem as a student? Would the administration have the time or inclination to work with you? Would they even care?

If your answer is, "Yes, this is my dream school and I still want to attend," then you need to think about finding another way to experience the school. Reach out on the internet forums or talk to other applicants you know. If the school won't see you alone, maybe they will see two of you. Maybe a current student will show you around one day. Maybe the admissions office will let you show up early for an Open House or stay a little late after it is over. None of these options are as good as an actual Scheduled Visit, but they are better than nothing.

Personal Experience

I am actually going to save this story for the end of the chapter, but to give you a quick summary of my experience with the Scheduled Visit: I scheduled a week-long road trip to coincide with the Open House I wrote about previously. I called all the big schools in Boston and I also called the New England School of Law and Vermont Law School to ask about scheduling visits.

The big schools gave me a variety of answers. One told me that it was unable to accommodate my request at all. Another reminded me to attend an Open House the school was hosting a few weeks later. A third told me I could take a self-directed tour by downloading a map off their website. The New England School of Law set a firm date with me for that Friday. Vermont Law School told me that they would always be happy to show me around and I could stop by anytime I wanted.

Different schools with different answers, and as I will tell you at the end of this chapter—I had distinctly different experiences.

Twenty Questions to Ask — The Art of Conducting the Visit

Okay, you have managed to get your foot in the door. Now what do you do?

I know I have said this before but everyone's experience is unique. Your questions and your concerns are only known to you. Take the time to think about what you would like to know ahead of time and you won't be lacking for questions to ask. In the meantime, here are some suggestions pulled from my personal experiences.

Disclaimer

There questions were some of the ones I asked when I was evaluating law schools. They are based on my personal preferences. By all means use them to help give you ideas about what to ask but try to come up with your own list of issues that matter to you.

---

01. Where do students live? Is there housing appropriate for your family? What is the average rent?

02. Are there food and entertainment nearby? How far will you need to go to get milk, bread, and a DVD rental? What about gasoline?

03. What about mass transit options? Where is the closest airport or train station?

04. What is the weather like? Is it too cloudy all the time? Is it too sunny? Is it too hot or too cold? Will you regret living here in the middle of January? What about the middle of July? Will you be dealing with hurricanes, blizzards,

earthquakes? Are you okay with that? (I had one friend transfer out of a California law school because he was completely freaked out by the two tiny earthquakes that occurred during his first semester. He probably would have benefited from asking himself these questions.)

05. Is there parking on campus? If not, how do people get to school—public transportation, walking, etc.?

06. What is your first impression of the overall environment like? Can you envision yourself attending school here? Does the vibe turn you on or off?

07. What is the accessibility of the administration like? Are you able to speak to the people you need to speak to? What about in an emergency?

08. What is the accessibility of the faculty like? Are they available to their students? Is there a mentoring program? What do the students have to say about access to their faculty?

09. What are the buildings like? Are they new or old? Are they suitable for your learning style? Do they have appropriate physical upgrades such as internet lines and electrical outlets?

10. Speaking of learning style, what are the classes like? How many students?

11. How are classes conducted? Do the students use laptops? Do the professors teach using the Socratic Method or alternate methods like

PowerPoint and seminars? Are you okay with that?

12. What are the bathrooms like? (The quality and cleanliness of a school's public bathrooms should tell you a lot about how well-maintained the school is on a daily basis)

13. Is there any construction scheduled in the near future? Will construction projects or building renovations have an effect on school operations during your time on campus?

14. Are you able to observe a class? If so, what is the attitude of the students? Are they happy, engaged, and responsive or are they distracted, disinterested, and demoralized? Is the professor, knowing he or she has an applicant observing the class, a jerk to the students?

Author's Note

I sat in on one criminal law class at a school that shall not be named where the professor asked me a simple question and then taunted a series of 1L students for knowing less than a new applicant. After confirming from those same students that the professor was indeed, a jerk, I promptly dropped that school to the bottom of my list. I was not going to pay one dime of that professor's salary so I could sit in class and be ridiculed. Frankly, nobody should.

---

15. Are you able to talk to some of the students? What are their stories? Do they seem happy or bitter? Why? Are they recommending the school or trashing it?

16. What extracurricular activities are popular on campus? Are these things in which you would be interested?

17. What is the socio-political culture of the school like? Is it far-left (e.g.: Berkeley) or far-right (e.g.: Regent University)? Do your interests align? If not, are you comfortable being in the minority?

Another Author's Note

My Italian-American friend Chris went to a HBC— Historically Black College – for his undergraduate degree. He told me that he thought he was prepared to encounter moments of casual racism and stereotyping on a campus where he was only one of a handful of non African American students, but he was overwhelmed with the frequency and hostility that often accompanied it. Although he graduated almost ten years ago, for better or for worse his memory of his college experience is dominated by the isolation that he felt while he was there. While not directly relevant to the question above, I thought his sense of isolation is similar to those who are represent the minority view in a community in other ways.

---

18. What is law school's recruitment support like? Does the school assist its students in finding summer work? What about after graduation? Does the school support its alumni after they have received their degrees?

19. What is the accessibility of the financial aid office like? Are you able to talk to someone in the office about your financial aid options?

What sort of financial support programs are available at the law school? How many people get scholarships and what are the criteria? Is work-study available? What about loan forgiveness after graduation?

20. What is the school's overall mission? Will you be happy here? Will you be successful here? Will you be able to translate your success at this school into a career after graduation? What is your gut telling you?

The questions you ask and the observations you make can go on and on. What is important is that you get the best possible sense of what your experience might be like at that particular law school. Much like when you buy a car, you must trust your instincts and avoid being distracted by flashy gimmicks. A law school might really hype its amazing third-year clinical program but what good is that to you when the clinic only takes ten students a year and the last incoming class had three hundred? Meanwhile, that same law school has no internet signal in the classrooms and you want to use an online commercial outline in class. You are ultimately the captain of your own law school experience. Visit as many schools as possible and learn as much as you can. The more information you can arm yourself with ahead of time, the greater the chance you will be able to identify the best law school for you.

Personal Experience: a Bad Visit in Comparison to a Good Visit

As I mentioned earlier, I took a trip to Boston to attend a law school open house. I attempted to schedule additional visits with several potential schools: a couple of schools in Boston as well as the New England School of Law (NESL), and Vermont Law School (VLS). NESL set a time of three o'clock in the afternoon on Friday, and VLS—those crunchy hippies—told me to stop by whenever I wanted.

Disclaimer

Unlike most of my recollections in which I offer my opinion on a school, I am not going to obscure the identities of these two schools for two reasons. For one, it is because my experience with NESL was so objectively bad that I feel it is totally fair for me to mention the school by name. For the other, it is because I ultimately decided to attend VLS, and the visit I had with the school was a very large factor in making that decision.

That said, you should still take my words with a few grains of salt. This is only my opinion and in no way reflective of what the schools are like today. My memory is good and I have tried to be as honest as possible in describing my recollections, but the reality is I visited NESL once and I have not been back in almost ten years. Nor have I been back to VLS since I graduated. For all I know, my experiences in visiting both schools represent statistical outliers compared to the experiences of most. My goal is not to vilify or promote either school. It is to provide you with a real world example of how important and effective school visits can be. I strongly recommend you research and visit each school yourself if these are two schools in which you are interested.

New England School of Law

I arrived at NESL a little early because the trip into Boston did not take as long as I thought it would. I noted the bustling downtown location of the school, but I appreciated that getting in and out of the city was still pretty easy. The Boylston tram station was only a block or two away. I took a moment to walk around the neighborhood—it had a sort of new urban downtown chic vibe to it—and then ducked into a coffee shop to wait until my appointment.

I had never been to NESL before. I had applied primarily because it was located in Boston (which would make my wife very happy). Also, the LSAT and GPA averages were pretty low, and I thought that made me a good candidate for a scholarship. I knew the school was located in multiple buildings in downtown Boston and that it had been founded as a law school for women shortly after the turn of the twentieth century. I also knew that NESL was a big supporter of experiential law learning and maintained a large number of clinics. Other than that, the school was a big blank page for me. I was completely open to loving it or hating it.

When I walked into the building, I immediately noted the security booth set up at the entrance along with a large but extremely bored looking security guard. Each person coming into the building had his or her identification checked and was required to sign in on a visitors' log. It was not exactly my idea of a warm welcome, but I can sympathize when a law school is located in a highly trafficked urban center.

I gave my name to the guard and he appeared to call the admissions office while I waited. I did not know it at the time, but the admissions office was not located in the same building as the library and classrooms. In fact, all of the administrative offices including admissions and financial aid were located in different buildings from the faculty and students.

There was very little traffic moving in and out of the building, and I spent my time reading the school's brochure again. After about ten minutes, I began to wonder if anybody from admissions was going to come get me. I asked the guard to call again. He said somebody was coming down. I continued to wait. I should mention that, to the best of my memory, there was not any place to sit down. It was not that sort of lobby.

About five minutes later, two young ladies came into the lobby. They were nice enough, but I would be lying if I said I could remember their names. Let's call them Anne and Beth. We all shook hands and they told me that they were second year students at NESL and had been asked by an admissions officer to give me a tour.

Anne did most of the talking. She spoke quickly and seemed to be constantly moving. Beth was much quieter but also seemed full of energy. They hustled me into the elevator and hit the button for the top floor. Anne gave me a thirty second summary of the school's ninety-five year history. It was quite similar to the one in the brochure, but she got most of the dates and a few of the names wrong. I nodded along and wondered where we were going.

Now, my memory is fuzzy, so I am not going to try to describe the layout with too much detail. Frankly, I do not remember the specifics. The building was five or six floors high. I remember that the top floor was upper level classrooms and the moot courtroom. The floor below that was dedicated to the faculty offices. Anne and Beth both told me that the floor was strictly off limits except for scheduled office hours. We did not get off the elevator, but I was permitted to stick my head out and look up and down the hallway.

The rest of the building was divided into the library (three floors) and first year classrooms (one floor). Anne, Beth, and I got off the elevator at the classrooms and proceeded to walk the entire length of the hallway. All the classroom doors were closed and all the lights were off. I asked if it was possible for me to observe an afternoon class and both girls laughed. No, they told me. Classes were done for the day. Apparently, there were no classes after three o'clock in the afternoon on that particular Friday.

Always moving forward, Beth opened a door to one of the classrooms while Anne described how the groups of students moved around the building during class changes. I do not remember the details but I do remember thinking it sounded very clever. We kept moving.

We moved floor to floor like that. Constantly walking while Anne kept up a high speed patter about the law school, classes, and the fact that spring break was next week. It was not until we hit the library and I saw a vast empty space with only a lone librarian sitting at a desk that I realized what Anne was telling me: It was Friday afternoon. Classes were finished. Spring break was next week. There was nobody left in the building. The school was essentially closed. Why the NESL admissions office had scheduled my visit at such an obviously terrible time to show off the school is a question for which I still do not have an answer. Maybe the lady I spoke to on the phone wasn't thinking or maybe she did not care. I have no idea.

I apologized to Anne and Beth for keeping them and asked if they had plans for the break. Yes, they told me. They were both flying home that afternoon. I asked them why they had decided to stay late to show me around. I cannot remember the specific reason, but obviously somebody in Admissions had grabbed them at the last second and charged them with showing me around.

I remember asking if they could just drop me off with the person in charge of admissions. Anne told me everyone in Admissions had already left. I asked about the Financial Aid office. Anne and Beth both told me they thought everyone in the administration was already gone for the day, and besides, all the offices were located in a different building from the one we were in. I walked with them to the lobby with the distinct feeling that I was getting the shove off.

Back in the lobby, the girls wished me good luck in the application process. They asked if I had any questions, but I could tell from their faces, anxious and pinched to be done with this last responsibility, that they really just wanted me to leave. My entire visit lasted less than thirty minutes.

I sat in my seat on the outbound tram feeling increasingly irritated and, frankly, a little disrespected. Here I was—a student whose LSAT and GPA scores put me head and shoulders above the average NESL student and that was how much the school valued me as a candidate. I had made the effort to drive all the way up to Boston. I had even called the admissions office to schedule the appointment and asked about the ability to observe a class and meet with someone from the admissions and financial aid offices. What did I get? Nothing. I got two overworked and unprepared students who just wanted to go home for spring break.

Was the school being intentionally rude or was it just poorly managed? Probably a mixture of both. I think that my LSAT and GPA scores implied to the admissions committee that NESL was most likely a safety school for me. That was one of the reasons I scheduled a visit. I wanted to show them that I had a real interest in NESL as a potential school for me. Of course, after that experience, I scratched the school completely off my list. It was unfortunate that I had already submitted my application because I essentially gave the school a $50.00 donation in the form of my application fee.

Almost ten years later and I still shake my head at the experience. I know that the NESL of today offers student-guided and self-guided tours as well as the opportunity for applicants to observe a first year torts class. The web presence of the school is also significantly improved. I do not know if these options were available back when I applied or if it was just that they were poorly advertised. The unfortunate truth is that if my experience visiting NESL had been better, it is likely I would have chosen to attend even if I had only received a partial scholarship. The location of the school and its focus on clinical programs were a big draw to me. Unfortunately, the cavalier way I was treated when I actually showed up led me to believe that I would never get the experience I wanted or needed from the school. I took my candidacy and my tuition elsewhere.

Vermont Law School

The following Monday, I drove up to Vermont.

Before I left, I called the admissions office to ask if they were on Spring Break that week as well.

"Nope," was the reply, "Come on up. Just be careful of the spring thaw. We call it the mud season. There's a lot of mud on the dirt roads and it's easy to get bogged down. Don't wear nice shoes."

After reassuring them that I was driving a big

pickup truck and had plenty of experience going 'mudding,' I hit the road and headed north. I did, however, change out of my suit and put on a pair of khaki trousers and some Timberlands. I was not sure what business casual should look like when combining a law school interview with Vermont springtime mud.

First, let me say that there are a lot of little intangible things that make an experience "a good experience" for a particular person. For me, the beauty of the Green Mountain state as the fog in the valleys was slowly burned off by the morning sun moved my very soul, but not nearly as much as the way Boston's rush hour traffic dropped away mile by mile. By the time I slipped across the border into Vermont, I only caught the occasional twinkle of chrome from another vehicle far ahead or far behind me on I-89.

There is little I hate more in this life than driving in the heavy traffic of an urban area. Naturally, I was in heaven.

I arrived in the small Vermont village of South Royalton shortly before noon. It sits on the west bank of the White River across a small bridge from Vermont Route 14. It is a small town laid out on a half a dozen streets and centered around a town square the size of a football field. There is a monument to the men of South Royalton who fought in the Civil War located by the bandstand. Between the bridge and the bandstand and covering the northwest quarter of town is the law school.

There are three or four newer interconnected buildings branching off from a beautiful Queen Anne's Victorian house that was the original law school building. It is now the admissions and administration building. The whole campus is small. Maybe ten acres that slope down gently to the banks of the White River.

I parked in the town square and walked back toward the law school. As soon as I turned at the break in a small picket fence that marked the pathway up to the admissions office, the door opened and a petite brunette woman poked her head outside.

"Hi," she said, "You're not J.D., are you?"

That was the beginning of my experience touring Vermont Law School. I could bore you with a thousand little details, but I won't. I will tell you that I was ushered into the Admissions office. I met with the school's Director of Admissions—a very nice woman who seemed generally interested in learning more about me and what I wanted to do with my law degree. I asked her my basic questions about class sizes and faculty participation. She answered honestly and without needing to dig around for the answer. I asked about financial aid and she told me that I would meet with the head of the financial aid office later in the afternoon. We discussed environmental law, for which VLS is consistently ranked number one in the country, and how specializing in that niche field has influenced everything about Vermont Law School from the advocacy and social awareness of the student body to the alumni's strong representation among the personnel of the Environmental Protection Agency.

Afterwards, I was taken over to the main building where I observed a 1L criminal law class. The lecture hall was open and airy with large windows that brought in a tremendous amount of natural light and minimized the need for the harsh fluorescent bulbs so commonly found in classrooms. The whole building had been built only a few years before. Its design and construction followed the environmental principals to which the law school had dedicated itself. Every feature from the passive heating design of the roof to the water-free composting toilets (not nearly as weird as they sound) was incorporated to minimize the building's environmental impact and carbon footprint.

The criminal law class was highly enjoyable. The professor was animated and the students were engaged. Everyone was taking notes on their laptops and several times the professor would reference supplementary source material found online. I was impressed with the seamless way VLS had already integrated technology into the classrooms and I appreciated that the whole building was already wired for Wi-Fi. Remember, I was applying at a time when schools were just beginning to talk about wireless networks. Most university IT departments had just finished hardwiring their campuses and were trying to catch their breath.

The secretary for the admissions office collected me after class and asked if I would like to have lunch with some students. She seemed to pick two 1Ls at random coming out of class and introduced me to both of them. When I expressed surprise that she knew their names, she smiled and told me that the average class size of VLS was only a little over a hundred students, so it was easy to get to know everyone just by being friendly. It was a nice touch, I'll give her that.

The two students introduced me to the classic Vermont lunch: a sub sandwich and a bag of chips from a deli just off the town square, and I spent the next forty-five minutes peppering them with questions. Much like the admissions director, they were open and honest about their experiences. They did not hesitate to tell me the positives of VLS—like the school's unique general practice program and the fact that VLS was centrally located near all the best skiing in New England. They were also very open and frank about the negatives of VLS—like the unfortunate reality that firms from Boston and New York never bothered coming that far north to recruit and that the school's recruitment and alumni employment office was not terribly helpful for most students.

We talked about winters in Vermont and driving on snow. We talked about the surprisingly high cost of living in Vermont and the fact that the rental market was very much supply-side driven. We talked about where everyone went to get groceries, gasoline, and beer and how so many students had dogs. It was a wonderful opportunity to hear from individuals going through the experience that I wanted for myself, and it reinforced my belief that school visits are critical when making a decision on which law school to attend.

In the afternoon, I was introduced to the head of the financial aid office. He had my application for financial aid on his desk when I walked into the office, and we immediately got down to business. He laid several charts out on the desk and walked me through the method his office used for determining the cost of attendance for incoming students. He showed me the projected increases over my second and third years and he gave me a final summary indicating the best guess estimate of what a Juris Doctorate from VLS would cost me. It was a very big number.

After explaining the cost, he walked me through how I would pay for it all. First, he told me I would qualify for a partial scholarship. Writing my total cost at the top of a sheet of paper, he subtracted the scholarship and showed me the remainder. Next, he told me that the federal Stafford Loan program would allow me to borrow $18,500 each year in subsidized and unsubsidized student loans. That came out to a little over $55,000, which he subtracted from my cost. Then he subtracted the approximate value of my work-study pay checks which I would be eligible to earn during the second and third years of law school (work-study is not available to first year students). After subtracting all these funding sources, he arrived at a final number of remaining debt. That number, while still high, was definitely much more manageable. This is money, he told me, which is covered by the student. What if a student does not have any savings? Not a problem, I was assured, private lenders are more than happy to step in and assist.

At the end of the day, I walked out of the financial aid office with a clear sense of how much an education at VLS was going to cost me, and how I was going to pay for it. I also had a strong understanding of what the school was like and how I would fit into the community.

For me, the entire experience was appealing. From the rural location and the environmental law focus of the academics to the socially active student body and the long, cold, snowy winters, I liked everything about Vermont. The more I thought about it, the more it felt like a perfect fit. As I drove back south, I knew that VLS was a school I could be happy attending.

Takeaway:

Get out there and make your visits! Prior to visiting, I thought I would love NESL and dislike VLS. The opposite was true. Nothing beats experiencing a school first hand.

What if Visiting Is Not an Option?

So, you have fawned over the brochures and carefully examined every photograph on the website. The professors are impeccably dressed, the students all have perfect teeth, and the campus is simply gorgeous. You think you have found the perfect school for you...but it is located all the way across the country. How are you supposed to visit?

While some form of the personal visit is definitely the preferred method of evaluating a school, there are options that can help provide at least some of the same background and information in situations where a visit is simply not feasible.

1. The Alumni Network

Most schools maintain a robust alumni network in the larger metro areas, if only because it makes things easier when fundraising season begins. It should not be difficult to reach out to a school's admissions office and ask them to put you in touch with a few alumni who would be willing to talk to potential applicants. In many ways, a recent graduate is a better source of information than current students because the recent graduate has the added experience of being on the post-graduation side of the school's program. If there is anyone that can talk about whether a school is financially worth it or not, it is the recent graduate.

2. The Online Forums

Online forums can be both the best and worst place to get information and opinions on the schools in which you are interested. I recommend you cautiously explore the larger, better known law school forums. The individual school threads are often populated with self-obsessed cynics and trolls frequently posting the most offensive and often inane vitriol like snakes in a pit, spitting in each other's eyes. That said, there can also be valuable information hidden among the posts if you are willing to sift through the chaff.

A better place to start might be the smaller, school-specific forums. Often times these are set up by the schools themselves on large commercial services like Google or Yahoo!. They are a place where applicants and newly admitted students can gather together and swap information.

3. Social Media Sites

Less reliable than school-specific forums, but also more likely to result in completely raw and uncensored opinions, are the social media sites like Facebook, MySpace (assuming MySpace survives past the publishing of this book), and LinkedIn. It is easy enough nowadays to set up groups where individuals with similar interests can gather. It is also easy to do a search of individuals listing a particular school in their biographical information. Why not check out who in your area is attending your favorite school, and then drop them a line to ask them what they think of it? There is no guarantee that they will answer—but nothing ventured, nothing gained, right?

CHAPTER EIGHT
RANKING YOUR FAVORITES, APPLYING THE FUNDAMENTAL THEOREM OF LAW SCHOOL HAPPINESS, AND THE REASON WHY STUDENT LOANS STINK

CONGRATULATIONS! IT IS almost the end of the summer. College football is in the air, and law schools all over the country are getting ready to release their applications. It might be hard to believe when you think about it, but you are almost done with the whole law school application process.

"But wait," you say, "I haven't done anything yet! I took the LSAT and I visited a few schools.

That's it! How can anyone think that I am almost done?"

Simple. It is because the most difficult part of applying to law school is the *search* for the right law school. Sure, you still need to fill out the applications, obtain some nice recommendations, and write a few high-speed, low-drag personal statements, but that stuff is child's play compared to the frequently imprecise and highly emotional process of whittling down the lists of law schools right for you.

Not only is this the hardest part, it is also the most *important* part because the school you choose to attend is going to define everything about your law school experience. The right school for you is the school that is going to support your intellectual development and mold you into a scholar of the law in an environment that feeds not just your mind but also your body and soul. Your experience as a student is going to inform your experience as an attorney and your experience as an attorney is going to have a huge effect on your clients, your family, and those closest to you.

So, since you have now taken some time over the spring and summer to visit various law schools (or utilized the other techniques we discussed in Chapter Seven), let's review your progress and timeline.

Takeaway:

The right school for you is completely independent of rankings or the opinions of family, friends, and coworkers. The right school for you is completely dependent on you.

By now you have completed the following: You have taken the LSAT. You have reported your GPA to the LSAC and your transcripts cover through at least the end of your junior year. You have taken your large initial list of possible schools and narrowed it down at least three times: the first time using your LSAT score, the second time using your cumulative GPA, and a third time through visits and open houses.

You should now have a nice, short list of potential schools; all of which meet your parameters for LSAT score and GPA and also seem, from your limited interaction, to be schools that match your needs, desires, and personality as a student. No doubt you have a couple of favorites in your list as well as a couple of schools about which you are a little more ambivalent. That is fine and completely normal. However, what you should not have are any schools you would not be happy attending if they offered you admission. There is nothing wrong with having a safety school, but having a safety school on your list is definitely not the same thing as having a crappy school on your list that you hate but you hold onto because you absolutely know they will accept you.

If you still have a crappy (for you) back-up school on your list, I urge you to drop it now. If that was the only school to offer you admission, then I can tell you now that you would not be happy there and you would probably serve yourself better by waiting to reapply next year. Do not worry; it will not come to that for the majority of those reading this book. For the few of you who are really concerned, I will discuss some of your options in Chapter Eleven. Regardless, let's rank your list from most preferred to least preferred. Remember: this book is not just about getting into law school. It is about getting into law school *cheaply.*

Ranking Your List — How You Put it all Together

1. Root for Your Favorites

The very first step in organizing your list of top contenders is to pull out the one or two favorites. If there are any schools there that you fell in love with when you visited, go ahead and rank them at the top.

2. Rankings Matter...Sort of

Do you have any schools ranked in the U.S. News top twenty-five? If so, add them to the next spots on your list below your favorites.

3. Rank by Cost

Finally, rank the remainder by order of average total cost of attendance.

I am guessing your first question is going to be, "Why do you rank schools based on cost? Aren't school rankings, job placement rates, or bar passage percentages a more worthy metric to rate schools?"

Well, yes and no. We are not following the traditional law school application dynamic. That has not worked particularly well for the majority of students in quite some time. It works extremely well for the top five percent who get into a top five school and then graduate in the top five percent of their class. For everyone else, the traditional method kind of stinks.

Let me walk you through what we are doing: our first goal was to have you strip out all the schools for which you were not qualified either because of your GPA or your LSAT score. We accomplished that back in Chapter Six. Once those were tossed out, we could focus on the schools for which you have a reasonable chance of getting accepted. Remember that you can always add back in one or two of those schools for which you did not make the LSAT or GPA cut. It is your life, and if you seriously want to give a particular school a shot, then we are all here to support you.

Once we had subjected your list to the harsh light of reality, then you did your research and made your visits. Hopefully, you found one or two schools that totally clicked for you. I think there really is a school out there for everyone, and I hope that you found yours.

Of course, that is not the end of the process, is it? While you might absolutely love the Superb University School of Awesome Law and that same school might fall squarely in between the left and right lateral limits as defined by your LSAT score and GPA, there are still two terrible possibilities. The first is that you get rejected. The second, and even worse possibility, is that you get accepted, but you receive no financial aid. Believe me, rejection sucks but it is not nearly as terrible as being so burdened by debt that you are never able to practice the law you want to practice. Instead, you are forced into a career of indentured servitude where you grind away for *literally* the rest of your adult life to pay off a debt you should never have assumed in the first place.

Do not freak out. You are not there yet. That is not going to happen to you. Remember, you are reading this book to learn from my mistakes. That puts you ahead of the game right from the beginning.

My point is that passion has its place, and if you have found your dream school, then absolutely put it at the top of your holiday list. If you are fortunate enough to have any top twenty-five schools in your list, go ahead and rank them next—but limit yourself only to the top twenty-five. Why? Well, the fact of the matter is that rankings only matter in the first half of the first tier (as determined by the U.S. News rankings). These schools are ranked so high and consistently attract sufficient recruiting attention that it might – and I heavily stress *might* – be worth borrowing the mindboggling large sums of money necessary to attend one of these fine institutions. Once you move out of the top twenty-five (frankly, once you begin moving out of the top ten), the value of one ranking over the other matters less and less.

Finally, you ranked the remainder by cost because at the end of the day, the cost of your education is going to dictate what sort of lawyer you get to be. Who cares what the bar passage rate is? If you study appropriately, you will pass it even if everyone else in your class fails it. Law school prepares you to study law. It does not prepare you to pass a bar exam. That is the job of a professional prep course like BARBRI, Kaplan, or BarMax and your own willingness to dedicate yourself to nothing else but studying for two months. Job placement rates are nothing but smoke and mirrors. Stories abound of law schools creating temporary work assignments for unemployed graduates just to avoid having to report a low placement rate. You are not going to worry about job placement rates for the rest of the school. You only need to worry about them for yourself.

If you saddle yourself with massive student loans, you will never be able to make your career chasing your passions. I can guarantee it. You will be locked into student loan payments six months after graduation that, at best, will exert a tremendous influence on your career choice, and at worst will crush you under the weight of a financial debt so heavy that you fall behind and find yourself fighting to explain why you should be allowed to continue practicing law even though you are a deadbeat.

Official Rankings and Why You Can Ignore Them

As we have discussed before, there is a misconception that rankings equate to happiness. That is to say, the higher the ranking of a school, the higher your relative happiness to be attending that school. I cannot stress enough that this idea is complete horse crap. Happiness and ranking have no correlation.

It is a misconception that rankings somehow equate to a quality law school experience. The assumption is that if you rank every law school from best to worst, you can show an incremental improvement in the quality of both the school and the student as you move up each spot in the rankings. While rankings may show a lot of things such as average LSAT score, average cost of attendance, average bar passage rate, and average percentage of alumni participation in fundraising campaigns, rankings cannot rank the quality of the law school experience.

Rankings are useful for providing all sorts of initial information on law schools for candidates and employers. Obviously, nobody should be looking at a law school that averages a three percent bar passage rate or costs five times the average tuition rate. Rankings are also helpful for providing a structure in which law schools can compete against each other and law school students can make themselves feel superior. That is about it.

The only people who need to pay particularly close attention to law school rankings are those individuals who have the LSAT score and the GPA that places them in the realm of the top ten. Rankings rapidly cease to have any importance as you descend the ladder from top ten to top twenty-five to top one hundred. Nobody knows the difference between attending the 49th ranked law school in the country and the 50th. Nobody is going to even be able to name the two schools ranked 49th and 50th without looking first.

Here is a little secret about Harvard, Yale,

Stanford, and the other top ten schools: Unless you want to clerk for a justice on the U.S. Supreme Court or become a first-year associate at one of the very large law firms on the east or west coast, attending (and especially paying for) a top ten school is totally not worth it.

They are like the cool kids clique in high school. They look awesome and they seem to get into all the best parties. Everyone wants to join them, but once you are inside (or once you have graduated), you realize they have all the same problems, issues, and moments of complete asinine idiocy as the rest of us. There is no benefit to attending one of these top schools except in the rare situations described above. You are far better off taking your brilliant mind elsewhere and winning yourself a full scholarship.

Takeaway:

Like so much in life, rankings only really matter if you are in the top ten. Unless you are applying to schools sitting at the top of the first tier, throw out the rankings and don't worry about them anymore. They are irrelevant to you.

Applying the Fundamental Theorem of Law School Happiness

Remember way back in the beginning of this book, I shared with you the fundamental theorem for law school happiness?

$(A / B) \times C =$ Happy Law Student

Where:

A = the sum total of the applicant's parts including grades, essays, LSAT score, and ability to perform at the level required for the study of law. In short, A = You. Unless you have a self-confidence problem, I would treat this as a constant.

B = the sum total of the parts of a particular law school in which the applicant is interested. This includes the school's average numbers for the LSAT and GPA as well as the school's bar passage rate, overall ranking and reputation. More importantly, this also includes the applicant's emotional connection to the school based on exposure (visits, alumni meetings, etc.)

C = the financial package available to the student.

I told you I would explain it in greater detail when you got to this chapter. The formula is not really meant to explain some complicated mathematical relationship that guarantees a single correct answer for each person. You won't feed your data into your calculator and come up with, "I must go to the University of Notre Dame." But you will gain a clearer understanding of the role that cost plays in determining your happiness. Read on for the full explanation.

You can plot all of the variables on a ten point scale and get a sense of how they interact. For context, let us assume that 1 is low and 10 is high. Now let us assume that you are a hard-working and highly intelligent candidate and you have applied and been accepted at three separate law schools: Perfect Fit University, Decent Fit College, and Horrible Fit School of Law. For purposes of this example, let us set the 'You' variable (A) at 10. After all, you are as prepared as possible to tackle the academic rigor of law school, right?

You get a variety of financial aid packages to include a full ride, half ride, and no ride (no financial aid). Let's see how the numbers shake out.

1. Perfect Fit University on a Full Ride, Half Ride, and No Ride would be:
(10 / 10) x 1 = 1
(10 / 10) x 5 = 5
(10 / 10) x 10 = 10

2. Decent Fit College on a Full Ride, Half Ride, and No Ride? Let's see:
(10 / 5) x 1 = 5
(10 / 5) x 5 = 10
(10 / 5) x 10 = 20

3. Finally, let's look at the numbers for Horrible Fit School of Law with a Full Ride, Half Ride, and No Ride:
(10 / 1) x 1 = 10
(10 / 1) x 5 = 50
(10 / 1) x 10 = 100

As you can see, the scale of numbers range from 1 to 100. Nothing beats Perfect Fit University on a full ride scholarship (total value of '1') and nothing is worse than Horrible Fit School of Law without any financial support (total value of '100').

Obviously, the ideal situation is being able to attend your dream law school on a full scholarship. Unfortunately, the reality is that full scholarship opportunities are difficult to obtain. However, you are much more likely to get some amount of a *partial* scholarship from the schools to which you apply. The hard part lies in determining which overall package is best for you. I want you to pay attention to the places where the values in our example above cross paths. For example; attending Perfect Fit University without any financial support carries the same numeric value as attending Decent Fit College on a half scholarship or attending Horrible Fit School of Law on a full ride.

I know what you are going to say, "But wait a minute, J.D. You have just spent the majority of this book repeatedly hammering the idea that I need to find a school with which I connect...that the law school *experience* is the most important thing to consider."

That is absolutely true, but the decision to attend a particular law school cannot be made in a vacuum. You must consider the economic reality that burdening yourself with student loan debt is going to have a substantial and near-permanent effect on the decisions you make for the rest of your life. Now is the time to make your peace with the idea that the cheaper you can obtain a quality legal education, the better.

Takeaway:

For every applicant out there, the sweet spot in the secret formula for law school application success is the intersection where the quality of the institution meets the cost. Ultimately, your degree is really only worth one thing: the right to sit for the bar in the state of your choosing. Go cheap. You will be happier in the long run.

Personal Note:

Although I had a wonderful experience visiting Vermont Law School, the financial aid package I received only gave me a 25 percent scholarship. I carried the bulk of the tuition and the associated costs of living in the form of student loans. When the time came to choose the law school I was going to attend, I turned down a full scholarship offer from a law school in California because, while my research gave me confidence that I would probably have been reasonably happy attending the school, my wife would have been miserable so far away from her family home in Massachusetts. Vermont seemed the best choice because it offered a good academic experience while being extremely close to my wife's family. I made the decision to commit to Vermont without considering the consequences that the student loans were going to have on my life. It seemed at the time that truly weighing the impact of the loans was somehow ignoble and unworthy of me. I mean, even if I ignored my wife's desire to be near her family, this was ultimately about the future of my legal education. Surely no cost is too high, right?

Five years after graduation, I am still over $100,000 in debt and my first marriage is long over. I can tell you now with absolute certainty that if I had applied the fundamental theorem of law school happiness as we discussed it above, there is no way the benefit of attending Vermont Law School would have outweighed its cost when compared to the full scholarship offer I had sitting on the table. They say hindsight is always 20/20, but all I know is that I grind my teeth a little harder every month when I send off that massive student loan check.

A Student Loan Bedtime Story, aka: The Ugly Reality of Student Loans

Once upon a time, college was fairly expensive and if you wanted to go to school, you needed to have one of three things going for you: family money, a merit scholarship of some sort (and possibly the discipline to work while going to school), or the willingness to join the military through one of the ROTC scholarship programs or by utilizing the G.I. Bill.

One day, the federal government had a really great idea. If loans for students were guaranteed by the government, banks would be much more willing to lend to students and then more people could go to college. This plan worked wonderfully well except for one small problem: the price of tuition suddenly started to increase.

Economists were amazed. It defied all logic. The rate of increase surpassed the federal interest rate, the rate of economic growth, even the rate of inflation. Strangely enough, the rate of increase seemed to keep remarkably close correlation to only one thing: the rate of increase in the borrowing rates of federal loans for students. As the federal program expanded its borrowing ceiling to provide relief to students, tuition rates would rapidly rise to close the gap. It was an economic phenomenon that boggled the minds of everyone except the young men and women who were doing the borrowing. They were reassured by the rest of society promising that college was always a good investment.

Eventually, the amount of money being borrowed by students became so large that some graduates could no longer be assured that they could get a job with a sufficiently high salary to cover the cost of repaying their student loans. Shockingly, people began to default on their student loans and the banks became scared.

"Help us, Federal Government!" said the banks, "We have grown used to the steady interest payments coming from our student loan recipients, but some of them aren't willing to pay their loans back, and a few are even trying to discharge their debt through bankruptcy!"

"Not a problem," said Congress, and passed a law prohibiting anyone from shedding their student loan debt through the declaration of bankruptcy. From that point forward, student loan debt stayed with an individual until it was fully paid off...or the individual died.

Meanwhile, the colleges and universities continued to increase their tuition and fees little bit by little bit every year. This allowed them to build lots of shiny new buildings and pay for massively bloated administrative staffs. They continued to sell students on the idea that a degree from their school would open up innumerable doors to a future filled with promise and fulfillment. Students kept applying and consequently, new graduates kept going deeper and deeper into debt. Who could have imagined a day when choosing to go to college would not be a smart investment?

Today, college has gone from being a fairly expensive investment in one's future to being an outrageously expensive investment and, for many people; the cost is too high. For hundreds of thousands of students over the past two decades, the burden of student loans has required them to forego the acquisition of all the different facets of the American Dream for which they had gone to college in the first place: a rewarding and fulfilling job, a spouse, a family, even a home of their own. The economic alienation of our generation is, without exaggeration, one of the most serious problems facing the future of the United States.

However, we cannot lay all the blame on Congress or the banks. A big part of the problem is us. As students, we have become so conditioned to believing that education is always worth the cost that it is very tough to resist the desire to borrow just a little more each year for a law degree. The fact of the matter is that there are really only a handful of institutions where the J.D. is worth the $150,000 you would need to pay—places like Harvard, Princeton, Stanford, and Yale. The recruitment of the best graduates from these schools remains strong even in the worst economies.

Even at those schools, the degree would only be worth it if you knew that you could perform at the level necessary to graduate near the top of your class *and* you knew that you wanted to work in one of the Big Law firms on the partnership track. If you have those qualifications and you already know that you want to pursue that work, then by all means borrow until your face turns blue. More power to you.

For the vast majority of us who will not be working in Big Law, the value of the degree is rarely worth the cost. We must measure the price versus the reward in order to come up with the most cost effective way to obtain our law degrees. That is the whole point of this book. I want you to not only gain admission to the best school for you, I want you to get as much scholarship money as possible.

It used to be that an applicant would go to the highest ranked law school on his or her list of acceptances. That is no longer the smart move. Today, an applicant should go to the "best fit" law school on his or her list that is also the most affordable.

Takeaway:

You must minimize the amount of student loan debt you take on. Do not get blinded to the name or rank of a particular school. It is far better to graduate debt-free from a Tier Four law school then to graduate with $150,000 in debt from a Tier One law school.

A Final Note on Your Law School List

This is a chapter filled with a lot of harsh truths. I will tell you right now that it is very important for you to come back and re-read this chapter in the spring or summer after you have received all the acceptance/rejection/wait-listed letters back from the schools to which you applied. While I wish you the very best luck in applying for admission, I am actually not terribly worried about your chances. If you followed my advice in taking the LSAT and appropriately narrowed your list of potential schools, I have no doubt you will do fairly well. Where I really want to wish you luck is in your financial aid applications. They are the real challenge.

When it is all said and done, I hope that you have the option of choosing to attend your "Perfect Fit University" on a full ride scholarship, but even if that is not a reality for you; I hope that I have given you a set of tools you can use to make the process of deciding a little more easy.

In the next chapter, we will be rolling up our sleeves and plunging into the nuts and bolts of the application process. All the little tips and tricks I learned for crafting the perfect application will be yours to use. I will also give you some important advice on hunting for scholarships and filling out the financial aid application. I will even tell you how to score the best recommendation letter ever.

So, when you are ready, take a deep breath and turn the page.

CHAPTER NINE
EIGHT THINGS TO KNOW ABOUT APPLYING

ONCE AGAIN, LET us examine your time line. By now it is the end of the summer. Perhaps you have been enjoying a respite from academia or maybe you have taken some summer classes (If so, it can't hurt to report those new grades to the LSAC!). Maybe you have been working a summer job. Maybe you have been out of school long enough that you have been working your normal job. In any case, I hope you have also found the time to visit a few of the schools on your list. If not then please don't think it is too late. While it is always better to visit a school before you apply, you still have the opportunity to visit after the applications are submitted. If you realize a particular school is a stinker for you, then at least you are only out the application fee.

There was one other thing I mentioned way back in Chapter Three that you needed to do during the spring and summer – download and review your preferred law schools' previous applications. If you have not done so yet, run to the closest computer and do it now. They are almost always available on the law schools' admissions page. If you cannot find them there, do a Google search. Usually at least one person each year will post a blank application on one or more of the law school forums.

Previous years' applications are a gold mine of critically important information for you. They are the Arthur Murray "footsteps-on-the-floor" dance lessons you get before the big date. The majority of applications, the majority of the time, change in no substantive way from year to year. Sure, the admissions committee might change the wording of a question here or there but the requests for substantive information remain the same.

Why should we think this is so awesome? Hopefully, this is already obvious to you but if not, then it is because you get the opportunity to take as long as you need to carefully construct the world's most perfect answer to every question on the application. It reminds me of that old kids' show on NBC, "Out of This World" where actress Maureen Flannigan could stop time. She could manipulate everything around her so that when she restarted time, it appeared that she had done something impossible like finishing her finals in just a few minutes.

You get to perform the same trick. You have months to prepare your application to law school before the application is even published. Not only that, you have the ability to submit your application, perfect and complete, almost immediately. The key is to know that all the questions you are going to be asked have already been asked in one of the recent years' applications.

Having the application questions in advance is great, but you still need to know how to answer them effectively. To that end, let us go through the top eight tips and tricks every applicant should know when filling out applications.

Disclaimer:

Although I have said this before, permit me to say it again: this is my opinion based on my experience and my knowledge. You are more than free to disagree or disregard anything you read here. Each application and each applicant is unique. There is no guarantee that what works at one school will work at another. As always, use your best judgment. Do not operate heavy machine while reading this book.

Collect and Read Old Applications

I covered this at the beginning of the chapter but I think it is important enough to place it at the top of the list. Think about it: law school admissions committees get to see your LSAT score, your GPA, a couple of recommendations and your application. From that very narrow window into your life, they need to make a decision on your suitability for admission to their school. Your application is the only part of your package in which the committee gets to "hear" your voice unfiltered.

The difference between success and failure usually comes down to practice. This is the only part of the application packet that you get to control from start to finish. Take the time to practice your answers until they are perfect.

Follow the Directions

I know, I know. People have been telling you this since kindergarten. Well, everybody says it because it is true. Nothing makes it easier to toss an application in the rejected pile than obvious problems with an applicant's ability to follow the required format or provide the necessary information. I am not even going to mention how fast committees trash applications that come in after the cut-off date.

Look, the ugly truth is that admissions committees are made up of human beings just like you and me. They get up, go to work, raise children, etc., just like everybody else. When they sit down every week in front of the massive pile of applications that make up their rolling admissions schedule, they attempt to make fair and impartial judgments on the quality and suitability of each applicant.

However, before they even waste a moment of their time looking at the content of your application, they are going to check to see if it followed all the directions. They will treat each breach of the instructions like a slap in the face. From their point of view, there is no excuse for it. As a result, you become labeled as either self-centered, disrespectful, or lazy. No matter what, from that point on you are fighting an uphill battle just to get past that initial prejudice.

Take the extra few minutes to read the directions and then make sure you follow them.

The Difference between Directions and Recommendations

On that note, let me take this moment to talk about the difference between directions and recommendations. You should treat directions like rules carved into granite. If the application requires that you submit a personal essay of less than one thousand words, then you need to trim your epic *Ode to the Supreme Court* down to 999 words and no "ifs", "ands", or "buts" about it.

You should treat recommendations like rules carved into a slightly softer material than granite. If a law school requires that you fill out at least one personal essay but recommends you submit no more than two, guess what? The admissions committee wants to see two essays. If you have only one really good essay to give them—that is fine. No problem. It's cool, man. They will still review your application, but if you think you're going to receive the same consideration and weight that the applicant with two well written essays is going to get, then you are crazy.

You need to have a really good reason (that is reasonably apparent) for why you cannot follow a recommendation. For example, many schools are now recommending that you submit their application online through the LSAC. Now, it is *just* a recommendation and the admissions committees will generally provide a mailing address for you to submit a paper application, but please do not think your application, which will look different from all the other applications submitted via the recommended way, will not receive unwelcome and unnecessary scrutiny, whether intentional or unintentional, unless you can find a way to neutralize it.

How do you neutralize your inability to follow a recommendation? Well, start by asking yourself why you aren't following the recommendation to begin with. Is it because you just really like Adobe Acrobat? Sorry, but that is not a good enough reason. Is it because your internet connection in the one room cabin you are renting while doing a senior internship with the Bureau of Land Management in North Dakota is too tenuous for you to efficiently utilize the online application form? Ooh, okay. Now you are cooking with gas. Not only is that an *excellent* reason why you are not following the school's recommendation, but it also shines a little light on an awesome part of your background.

How do you create the opportunity to provide the explanation? Simple. A short note attached to your application when you send it in should be all you need to explain yourself, remove the "taint" of being different, and even elevate your application into something special and different from all the others.

Grammar and Spelling Matter

Do we really need to go into any great depth on this issue? Nothing is going to paint you as a waste of the admission committee's time faster than misspellings and poor grammar.

Spelling matters. If you cannot turn in a document free of errors, you should not be applying to law school. It is not just a matter of running the spellchecker. You also need to make sure you can catch the little errors like "witch" versus "which" and "there" versus "their". Nobody is perfect so make sure you review your writing carefully and, if necessary, ask someone else to provide a pair of fresh eyes.

Equally important, make sure your grammar is up to par. If you have any doubts, refer to a grammar guide like *The Blue Book of English Grammar* or *The Elements of Style*. If there is a choice to be made between two accepted rules, pick one and be consistent throughout all of your writing. Again, I recommend you pick somebody you trust to read your writing with a focus on your grammar.

Don't Forget the Subtle Art of Presentation

There is an art to how your application is presented. It would behoove you to treat the application like it is your own personal Academy Awards production. There is not one single aspect of the Oscars that is not meticulously planned and presented. You should be able to say the same thing about your applications.

If you are submitting online, then take every opportunity to make sure that you formatted the answers properly and with an eye toward the aesthetic presentation. How does it look when it is printed on paper? That is how the admissions committee will see it. Make sure it looks as nice as possible.

Paper applications should be populated directly from Adobe Acrobat. If you do not have access to Acrobat, then you need to find someone who does or download one of the free trial offers. There is no excuse, in the collective mind of the admissions committees, for an applicant to be turning in a handwritten or typed application. Oh sure, they won't actually say something like that, but you better believe they are thinking it.

We could spend pages going through all the little details of how to create your application but I think you have enough to get the general idea. This is the presentation of 'you' to the committee. It should be perfect. Everything from the quality of the paper to the darkness of the printer ink to the size of the envelope you use has a direct or indirect effect on how the members of the admissions committee perceive your application (and consequently, how they perceive you).

A well-presented application package is not going to make a difference if an individual is woefully under qualified, but it will give a candidate an edge over every other equally qualified individual.

The first time I applied to law school, my applications were handwritten and unprepared. I was rejected by all but one school. The second time I applied, my applications were meticulously created using my graduate program's computer lab. I printed them on heavy-bond paper using a fresh printer cartridge. I signed them with a fresh black ink pen (and yes, I practiced my signature beforehand). I mailed them in large business envelopes that required no folding and I chose the most professional stamps I could find in my local U.S. Post Office. In short, I tried to control every aspect of how my application was received and perceived by each and every person on the admissions committee.

Give Yourself Time to Answer the Short Questions

Every law school is different. Some request that a candidate answer a series of short questions. Others want to mix short questions with longer essays. Topics will generally center on issues related to a candidate motivation or suitability for the study of law. While I cannot give you specific advice, I can tell you that you already have the one thing you need to successfully answer these questions: time.

By obtaining old applications early in the process, you have all the time in the world to allow the questions to percolate through your mind. Take your time in preparing your answers. Write out multiple answers. Explore your creativity. Allow others to read and comment on your answers. It is possible they can provide insight or direction that you would not have thought of yourself.

Remember: the admissions committee is a group of

people just like you and me. They want to see you answer the question in a competent manner that exhibits a high degree of writing skill and personal insight. They will see right through hyperbole and the non-answer answer faster than you can write it. Do not worry about impressing them. You already have the tools available and you have given yourself a tremendous advantage in time by preparing early. Do not procrastinate. Allow yourself the room to write and rewrite over and over again. Before you know it, you will find that you have created your perfect answer.

Give Yourself More Time to Answer the Personal Essays

I debated combining tips five and six together because so many law schools nowadays are merging their short essay questions and their long essay questions together. Some schools are only asking for one essay. Others are asking five short answer questions. Others have stopped asking a question at all and are recommending instead that each applicant, "...submit a personal statement that addresses some issue the applicant would like to bring to the attention of the admissions committee."

Wow, talk about giving you enough rope to hang yourself with!

These essays are the one opportunity for you to speak in your own voice to the admissions committee. Do not waste it.

Again, your best asset is time. You have all the talent and skill you need locked up inside you. It is time to let it out. Treat the whole process like a writing exercise. Write out answers to every question. Write them out again. Write them out in iambic pentameter. Write them from the point of view of a nineteenth century vicar or a twenty-third century space overlord. Do whatever you need to do to write, clearly and concisely, from the heart.

Remember that time is your friend in this exercise. If you start tripping over your own feet (metaphorically, of course), take the time to step away from your writing and regain your bearings. Do not forget to utilize the people around you to give you feedback.

Character and Fitness–How to Reveal the Skeletons in Your Closet

I am assuming that the end goal for everyone reading this book is to ultimately become an attorney. In order to be accepted into the bar of whichever state you apply, you will need to do three things. First, you will need to be able to pass the bar exam as well as the MPRE, MBE, and possibly other standardized tests. Second, you will need to be able to pay the bar dues. Third, you will need to pass a character and fitness background check.

That's right—a background check. Lawyers are a unique type of professional (as compared to doctors or business professionals) because lawyers are presumed to be honest and honorable officers of the judicial system. The courts do not, as a matter of course, want to allow liars, thieves, and criminals the ability to represent clients before the bar. The stakes are too high—not just for individual clients but for society as a whole.

What does this mean for you? Well, every law school application is going to have a Character and Fitness section that is going to ask you, with varying degrees of specificity, whether you have ever been in trouble with prior academic institutions, the legal system, or the military. Obviously, this is a highly personal question and it may be that you have had some issues in your past that you do not really want to rehash. If that is the case, I want you to know two things.

First: Whatever incident you are worried about is almost never as big of a deal as you think it is.

Second: You *absolutely* must disclose it.

Do you understand? If not, go read the two sentences above again.

The simple truth is that a substantial number of applicants have something in their past of which they are anything but proud. Whether you received a drunk and disorderly misdemeanor conviction during your undergraduate school's homecoming or were expelled for plagiarizing a mid-term paper, nobody actually cares. The admissions committee is not going to make a snap decision on your character and fitness because you disclose an indiscretion. What they *are* going to do is look at the severity of the incident, the time that has passed since the incident occurred, and your commentary on the resolution of the incident.

The most important thing to remember here is that you cannot lie. You cannot write that something similar but less severe happened. You cannot write that the outcome was different than it was. You cannot do anything except tell the complete truth. The issue is not that the law school might discover your deception (although it might), it is that the bar examiners, three years from now, will definitely discover the incident. Once they do, they will immediately pull your law school application to see if you disclosed it when you applied. Law school admissions committees and bar examiners can forgive almost anything, but you bind their hands with titanium handcuffs the moment you lie.

A Hypothetical Situation

A common example is a misdemeanor arrest for marijuana possession during your college years. First, let's look at what happened. As a freshman in college, you were busted with a joint during the homecoming football game. You were arrested, taken to the police station, processed, and bonded out on your own personal recognizance. You appeared before a magistrate a few weeks later and you pled guilty to personal possession. The judge fined you a couple hundred dollars, ordered you to do ten hours of community service, and gave you thirty days of jail time suspended. You went back to school properly chastised, worked your community service hours at the local soup kitchen, and have stayed on the straight and narrow ever since.

Okay, so the first thing we need to assess is the length of time since the incident occurred. You are submitting these applications around the first day of October in the fall of your senior year (or later) and your arrest occurred in the fall of your freshman year. It has been roughly three years since the incident. That is good. The more time between your incident and your application, the more room there is for you to show that you corrected the behavior or changed the environment that provoked the incident in the first place. Equally important, the more time that has passed, the greater the opportunity to show that your current maturity has replaced the immaturity that allowed your past indiscretions to occur.

Now let us look at the incident itself. What you did

was possess a personal amount of an illegal substance. In particular, you had a substance, the illegality of which, is subject to some measure of public scrutiny and the use of which is subject to much social debate. You were not harming anyone and the crime itself did not involve deception. This is a good thing. Issues of deception are difficult to discuss because the root problem of dishonesty is anathema to the purposes of the bar (as a lawyer, you are trusted to be telling the truth). In cases involving deception, time is your best friend—the more, the better.

To summarize: what you ultimately have to disclose is a crime that occurred when you were barely above the age of maturity, affected no one but yourself, was leniently adjudicated by an appropriate official, has not been repeated (thereby showing a trend of illegal behavior), and has had no detrimental effect on your undergraduate career. Not really that big of a deal, right?

My last piece of advice on this topic: do not be petulant or argumentative. Do not assign blame to anyone other than yourself. Be contrite, honest, and forthright. Accept responsibility for your actions and explain how you changed since the incident. The admissions committee is going to make its decision based on the totality of the material in front of it. All you can do is present the issue with complete and total honesty. In the end, that is really all you can do anyway. Any attempt at deception on your part is doomed to fail either now or when you apply for the bar, and ultimately lying now says more about your character and fitness to be an attorney and a person of integrity than any past indiscretion you might have committed.

It is All about the Money–Submitting the Financial Aid Package

The often ignored twin of the law school application is the law school financial aid application. Fortunately, you have me to tell you now that this application is just as important to fill out completely and competently as the actual application for admission. As we have discussed before, getting into law school is not that hard, but getting into law school without having to pay for it is still quite a challenge.

There is only one major rule that you need to remember about financial aid: The early bird catches the worm. What do I mean? I mean that there is only a limited pot of money every year and a huge number of students attempting to get a piece of it. Get your financial aid application in as soon as the school will accept it. Get your scholarship applications, if any are available, into the financial aid office as soon as possible. Always, always, *always* strive to be the very first in line.

There are four components of the financial aid process that you want to make sure you cover for each school to which you apply: the school-specific financial aid application, the Free Application for Federal Student Aid (FAFSA—which can be located at www.fafsa.ed.gov), your annual tax records, and any scholarship applications for which you think you might be eligible. Let's touch on each one briefly so you have an idea of what you need to accomplish.

School-Specific Application

The financial aid application for each school is generally released at the same time or shortly after the application for admissions. The sooner you return it to the school, the sooner you mark your place in the financial aid line. It is a simple form. Don't worry if you do not have all the information. The schools will be able to pull the additional information from your tax forms and FAFSA once you file them.

FAFSA

The FAFSA is the standardized form used by the federal government to administer the federal student loan program. You will need to register for the site and get your online PIN code. The PIN will allow you to log onto the site, sign forms electronically, and make payments after you have graduated. You can register for the site at any time but the new FAFSA becomes available after the first day of January every year.

Get the FAFSA done as soon as possible and make sure you designate the schools to which you have applied on the list of institutions that have access to your forms. I made that mistake once when I was hurrying to fill out the FAFSA one year and forgot to designate any schools. It almost cost me several thousand dollars in financial aid.

Annual Tax Filing

Your federal tax forms may be the most important financial aid documents you create every year. Hopefully, by the time you begin the process of applying to law school you have also finished the process of weaning yourself off your parents' (or other designated guardian's) financial teat. This is important not only because we all want to see you stand on your own two feet like an actual adult, but also because your impoverished condition as a financially independent student will make you that much more attractive to the financial aid and scholarship gods.

Your parents might resist. After all, they have

supported you for your entire life. Also, they get a pretty fat deduction on their taxes if they claim you as a dependent. If this is the case for you, and your parents are resisting your desire to file your own taxes this year, you need to have a very serious conversation with them. First, tell them that you love them and you appreciate everything that they do (and have done) for you. Second, tell them that it is incredibly important to your long term financial health that you qualify for as much scholarship money and therefore take as little student loan debt as possible—far more important, in fact, than the benefit they will get from claiming you as a dependent. If that does not sell them, then the third thing you tell them is that it is not their choice, you *are* filing your own 1040 this year whether they like it or not, and that if they try to claim you, the IRS will immediately note the use of your social security number on two separate tax filings and will likely, metaphorically speaking, beat them down like the woodsman's fairytale step-children.

Obviously it should go without saying, but you should file your taxes as soon as possible. These are not the years to wait until April 15th. Keep nice, clean copies for your own records and for sharing with any law school that requests them.

Once your FAFSA and taxes are complete, check to see if your law schools' financial aid offices want copies. They will most likely have already requested them from you, but it can never hurt to offer. Plus, it gives you the opportunity to call the office, charm the person answering the phone and, even in a very small and casual way, associate your name with good manners and initiative.

When you send your forms, make sure you include a cover letter. If you choose to redact any information, like your social security number, be neat about it. The envelope and any stamps you use should be similar to what you used when you mailed your applications. Everything you send should exude a sense of understated professionalism.

Other / Private Scholarship Applications

These are so unique and specific to each school and candidate that I debated not including them in the summary. The fact is that there are literally hundreds of scholarship opportunities out there for students who meet one of any number of criteria. From grades, to essay contests, to the willingness to dedicate oneself to a career of equine-related legal services, scholarship money is just floating out there waiting for the right person to come along and snatch it up.

Most of these scholarships are small awards ranging from $500.00 to $1000.00. Of course, winning even a few of them could have a major impact on your student loan debt. It is entirely up to you and your willingness to put the effort into finding, examining, and then applying to these sorts of scholarships. Check out the businesses you frequent as well as past employers. Look at your parents' employers. Often, corporations provide scholarships to employees, former employees, and the children of employees. Basically, look under every nook and cranny. If you have a relationship with a business or an institution, check to see if they have any scholarship money. It can never hurt to ask.

My advice is to focus on the big fish and then work your way down the food chain dependent on how much time you have available. Check to see if any of the schools to which you are applying offer merit-based scholarships. While consideration for these scholarships is often included when you submit your financial aid application, you should check to make sure you do not need to provide any supplementary forms or information.

If you remember anything, remember this: it is all about battling with a million other potential students for a very finite pool of resources. Be early and be thorough. The money you accrue through grants and scholarships is worth two to three times its value in student loans. Why? Because every dollar you borrow in student loans is a dollar you need to pay back. Borrowing $150,000 at 6.8 percent interest over a 25 year repayment period results in you paying back *over* $312,000 before the loan is finally retired. Ignoring the fact that nobody should still be paying student loans when they are turning 50, surely you will have other plans over the course of your life that might benefit from that extra $162,000—a house, your retirement, or your own kid's college tuition, perhaps?

When to Use Early Admission instead of Regular Admission

Most law school applications become available sometime in the month of September and have a deadline somewhere in February or March. It is important to remember that a deadline is just that: a DEADline. You will not be waiting anywhere near that long to submit your applications. Thanks to your hard work and preparations over the summer, you will be fairly well equipped to fill out the applications and return them with a minimum of delay. If the application is available on September 15th, you are mailing it back by September 19th. If another application is available October 1st, you will have it submitted by October 4th. I am sure you get the drift. You should not allow more than seventy-two hours to pass between the opening of the application season and the submission of your application packet.

Getting your application in first provides a multitude of benefits. For one, it shows that you are serious about a particular school. For another, your application competes against a minimum number of other candidates at a time when there are a maximum number of spots available. For a third, your application has the full amount of time to be considered by the admissions committee in the event that you are not accepted after the first review.

So, we have established that you will be getting all of your applications in as soon as possible, but what do you do about the schools that want you to designate whether your application is an Early Admission, Regular Admission, Early Restricted Admission or one of a dozen other synonyms for a preferred admission program? The answer to that question lies in a careful examination of the schools to which you are applying and the order in which you have ranked them.

If your number one choice offers some form of early restricted admission – where you commit to attend the law school if you are accepted – then go ahead and apply for it. The school is your number one choice, after all. If you get in, you are most likely going to attend. If any of the other schools on your list offer early restricted admission, make sure you steer clear. However, if any of the other schools on your list offer an early admission choice that is NOT restricted or obligating in any way, then you should definitely designate your application as such. It is like a free bonus for you. Each school treats your application like you prefer it over all others, but you have no obligation to actually follow through. There is no downside from your point of view.

Takeaway:
Always submit your applications as soon as you can. Always apply early admission if the option is available. Never apply early restricted admission unless the school in question is your very absolute first choice.

Using an LSAT Prep Company to Prepare Your Application

It seems like this is an industry that has suddenly sprung up in the world of law school applications in just the last few years. I think that in an attempt to diversify their revenue streams, LSAT prep companies realized that there was an untapped market of law school applicants desperate to pay anybody with the appearance of knowledge and authority to help them get into law school.

I cannot comment on the actual quality of any particular company, except to say that it seems to me that the law school application process is not particularly arduous or complicated and the parts that are, like the LSAT, are not the parts with which an advisor can really assist you. I think paying has the potential to be a colossal waste of money, but if an applicant wants a steady flow of reassuring feedback and the externally-provided guidance of an authority figure constantly reminding him or her of the approaching deadlines and requirements, then I guess maybe a professional application advisor might be just the thing.

In a Nutshell

So there you have it: applications and recommendations in a nutshell. My friends all thought I was a little anal-retentive when it came to preparing my packages, but I subscribe to the theory that anything worth doing is worth doing right. As a result, I received affirmative responses from more law schools and more financial aid offices than any two of them combined.

I have no idea how much of an impact each individual tip mentioned in this chapter will have on your applications, but I think the cumulative effect will be substantial. Certainly, I feel confident telling you that only a fool would miss the opportunity to exert even the tiniest positive influence on his or her application package.

Congratulations, by the way. If you are re-reading this chapter, then at this point your application packages have been submitted and your recommendations are on file with the LSAC. You have submitted the financial aid paperwork and you are waiting for the turn of the year to tackle the FAFSA and your federal tax returns. We will check back in with you in Chapter Twelve as you begin collecting your acceptance letters.

Chapter Eleven is going to deal with those applicants who have always had their hearts set on a particular law school but failed to get the numbers they needed. If you wanted to go to a certain school but under-performed in the LSAT, or in your cumulative GPA, or even in something else, then what can you do? To put it bluntly, you have three choices: quit, settle, or try again. We will examine all these options and discuss a few tips that might make you a better candidate down the road. However, let's first take a look at Chapter Ten and a quick guide on how to obtain the best recommendation letters possible.

CHAPTER TEN
HOW TO SCORE THE BEST RECOMMENDATIONS POSSIBLE

T HE LAW SCHOOL recommendation is probably the least important part of the application package. As long as the recommendations are present in the paperwork and as long as the recommender does not throw the applicant under the bus in his or her recommendation letter, most admissions committees read the recommendation letters as a sort of sanity check on the applicant and move on to the other parts of the application. 99 percent of the recommendations say exactly the same thing:

> Applicant X is a wonderful person who has performed very well in my classes. He or she has never been anything less than a joy to teach. He or she engages in meaningful debate and shows all the necessary acumen to be an attorney at your law school. I completely recommend this student.
> Sincerely,
> Prof. Y.

The example above is not a bad recommendation. Nor is it a good recommendation. It is an *adequate* recommendation. It says nothing negative and provides a sufficient measure of fluffy but non-specific praise. Reading between the lines, the admissions committee will read this recommendation as, "I am writing this recommendation because it is part of my duties as a college professor and I have nothing negative to say about this student." It is a neutral recommendation—one that causes no harm while also providing no benefit.

Much like the problem of grade inflation, recommendation letters have become bloated with hyperbolic praise such that it is insufficient to say just what you mean and still have an effect. Admissions committees will see the use of basic language as the technique of a recommender who feels unwilling to say anything negative while not wishing to provide actual positive praise. The best way to avoid this is the use specific examples, but most recommenders do not bother to take the time to provide examples on their own and most applicants do not know how they need to give their recommenders that level of support.

The act of requesting a recommendation creates a unique dynamic. On the one hand, you are asking a favor of an individual you respect and value. On the other hand, the recommender often feels obliged to say 'yes' even if he or she does not necessarily believe you deserve a good recommendation. Equally unfortunate; most applicants do not know that it is perfectly acceptable to take a strong and active interest in the timeliness and quality of the recommendation.

There are three types of recommendations you can receive. The most common by far is the neutral recommendation as displayed above. It is also possible that you can receive a negative recommendation—which can cause substantial damage to an applicant's package—or a positive review, which sometimes (but not always) can make you stand out from a crowd of otherwise equal candidates.

But wait, I know what you are thinking: How in the world could someone allow a bad recommendation to make it into the LSAC file? Who could possibly let that happen?

Unfortunately, there are a variety of ways a bad recommendation can make it past an unsuspecting student's radar. The individual picked to write it could have a negative opinion of the student's academic qualities while still liking the student as a person. The recommender could be unseasoned in the art of writing recommendations and therefore inadvertently damned you with faint praise. The recommender could make a mistake in something simple but critical to displaying their personal knowledge of your qualities. I am thinking of situations where a professor spells your name wrong or misidentifies your major or otherwise provides a piece of data incongruous with something else in your application.

So, what can you do? The simple answer is that you can write your own recommendations. Nobody knows you better than you, and nobody is more invested in your success than you. Obviously, I am not saying that you create "fake" recommendations from "fake" recommenders. What I am saying is that this is an opportunity for you to take firm control of your recommendation letters and insure that the very best recommendations possible are submitted to your law schools. Just follow the process below.

Who Can Provide the Best Recommendation?

This is not as difficult of a question as you might think. Who are the mentors in your life? Who are the individuals who inspire and motivate you? Who do you respect? With whom have you developed a connection or relationship that is deeper than just the formal professional relationship? These are the individuals you want to ask. They might be professors at school or supervisors at work. They might be important men and women in the legal, business, or religious community. It does not matter. You want to pick people who know you, even just a little bit.

As a general rule, status is valuable here. Among the list of individuals who meet the criteria above, most applicants would pick the ones with impressive job titles. I am not trying to be elitist or crass here. I just want to be honest. As a society, we value the opinion of people we consider important more than those of people we consider less important. However, status should not trump specificity when it comes to your recommendation letters.

Here is an exercise you can do at home. Pick which one is the preferred recommendation writer for you.

— Arch Bishop Thomas O'Brien, Catholic Arch Diocese of Big State, USA
or
— Pastor Tommy O'Brien, Friendship Church in Little Town, BFE

— Dr. Salvatore Romano, Director of Romantic Languages at the University of Awesomeness.
or
— Mr. Sal Romano, Owner and Operator of Sal's Pizza

— Judge Angela Johnson, Big State Appeals Court
or
— Ms. Angie Johnson, Supervisory Paralegal for Dewey, Cheatham, and Howe, LLP

— Mr. Nathanial P. Dexter, Senior VP of Investor Relations for International Conglomerate, Inc
or
— Mr. Nate Dexter, Day Shift Supervisor for McBurger Franchise #1289, Little Town, BFE

Let me guess—everyone picked the first of the two choices, right? Sure you did, and we all know why: Because perceived social importance carries an intrinsic value with which you want to associate yourself. Your recommender is someone important therefore you must be someone important.

Except, the first choice is not always the best choice. Certainly, it can be but it does not always have to be. The real importance is found in what the recommender says in the recommendation and not the title he or she puts at the top.

If Sal Romano, owner of Sal's Pizza, can speak with authority about your dependability, intelligence, and natural leadership skills, *and* if he can relate a few specific examples about how you hired and supervised all his other employees, *and* successfully managed the restaurant's appeal for a zoning variance from the local zoning board...well, that recommendation is going to beat the pants off the generic, non-specific recommendation coming from the highly esteemed Dr. Salvatore Romano.

Understanding that depth matters, we can now segue to the next step.

What Do You Want Your Recommender to Say?

The most fundamental purpose of the recommendation is to recommend you to the law school. If it is coming from a professor, you want it to talk about your academic abilities and your discipline. If it is coming from a supervisor at work, then it should talk about your dedication to your job, your competency as an employee, and your leadership or management skills. If it is coming from a personal friend or social contact, then it should talk about your character and fitness. If it is coming from a lawyer, a judge, or another member of the bar, it should discuss your legal acumen and potential for success as an attorney. Once you have determined who you want to have writing a recommendation for you, you need to determine if they can speak effectively to these particular areas of your personality. If you think they can, great. Now it is time to ask them if they will.

How to Pop the Question?

I am a big fan of the well crafted e-mail, but I think this is a question you can ask in either written or verbal format depending on your relationship and the frequency of contact you have with the potential recommender. For example, a professor you see four times a week and with whom you have a close and on-going mentor/mentee relationship? You could just ask him or her directly. But if it is a work supervisor with whom you have only occasional and professional contact, then you should send a formal e-mail request. In either case, what you ask for is more important than the method in which you ask.

Asking for a recommendation is a two stage

process. In the first stage, you ask the question and then give the reviewer time to think about it. In the second stage, you come back and get a yes or no answer. This works extremely well in weeding out those individuals who said yes immediately simply because they have a tough time saying no. It allows them time to come up with a reason to turn you down gracefully and avoids the situation where a recommender says yes to your face and then writes a half-hearted or even a detrimental recommendation letter.

You should be direct and to the point. Tell the potential recommender that you are applying to law school and would appreciate it if he or she would consider writing a recommendation for you. Tell him that you do not mean to put him on the spot. He does not need to say yes or no right now. Tell him that you would appreciate it if he could think about it for a day or two because this is an important part of the application process. If he feels that this is something he would like to do for you, he should tell you so when you ask him about it again in a few days. You will provide the recommender with everything he needs to complete the task. If not, for whatever reason, he should just let you know and you will ask someone else. Your feelings, relationship, quality of work, etc., will not be damaged by the refusal.

Create Your Own Recommendation Packet

Here is where it all comes together. You see, while the recommender is the one who is ultimately going to sign and submit the recommendation, you are going to do the majority of the writing.

Remember when I said you needed to be a good writer to succeed in law school? Well, here is your first chance. You will write your own dream recommendation for each recommender. Knowing yourself far better than anyone else knows you, write exactly what you wish your recommender would say about you. Make sure it is clear and concise and also filled with the sort of specific examples that are going to show an admissions committee that your recommender knows you well.

After you have written the world's most perfect recommendation for yourself, you need to create a companion summary sheet. Think of this as the recommender's cheat sheet. At the top, list your full name, address, birth date, undergraduate major – basically all the specific information about you that could conceivably be mentioned by a recommender. Next, list the theme of the recommendation. This will vary depending on the recommender. Underneath the theme, list the specific examples you provided in your dream recommendation. If there were other examples that you chose not to use, throw them on the end as well.

Finally, get the envelopes and stamps you will need and make sure everything is pre-addressed. Write up a brief guide on what to mail and where to mail it. Make everything as simple as possible for the recommender. Put it all in a folder and put your recommender's name on the outside. Now you are ready to go!

Deliver Your Packet and Follow Up

At this point, you have your packet ready to go and your potential recommender has had the opportunity to decide whether or not he or she feels capable of writing you a recommendation. If the answer is yes, then you are in a position to immediately give the recommender the packet at the time of your follow-up question. Do not worry if you have not completed the packet; just tell the recommender that you will give him some paperwork tomorrow that he will need to have, and then make the completion of the packet your priority.

Your key to success here is that you do not simply give the recommender the packet and thank him for his time. You need to walk him through the entire process piece by piece. You are actually selling him on a whole recommendation process and, at the same time, establishing that you will keep ownership and authority over your own recommendations. After all, this is your life we are talking about here.

First, show the recommender the pre-addressed envelopes and mailing instructions. Give him a brief overview of where the recommendation goes and how each law school ultimately gets a copy. This is assuming you aren't asking for school-specific recommendations. If so, it is not a problem—the process is very similar, but you will need to make sure the recommenders follow the directions for labeling a recommendation as school-specific.

Next, show the recommender the summary sheet. Explain that for his ease in preparation, you have provided a sheet with important information that he can reference. Tell the recommender that you understand how difficult it can be to remember specific information about every student that asks for a recommendation. Stress to him that he should feel free to use or not use your examples as he sees fit.

Finally, show him the sample recommendation that you wrote. Explain that this is only an example of what you would like to see. However, this recommendation is ready for a signature should the recommender find it easier just to sign and send.

Make sure to thank your recommender for his time. Remind him that your contact information is readily available on the summary sheet you provided, and that he can reach you any time if there are any questions. Tell him that you will be following up with him in a predetermined amount of time (usually one to three weeks but it is entirely up to you and your application schedule), and that you hope he understands you will be following up only because you know how busy the recommender can get. With that final flourish, gracefully withdraw and allow your recommender to get about his day.

The benefit of this method is that it utilizes the natural tendency of people to procrastinate. Your recommendation is very important to you but not very important to anyone else—including your recommender. If he feels appropriately motivated to write a recommendation, you have already provided a readily available list of facts and specific examples for his use. If he inevitably allows the days to slip by without writing the recommendation, then you have created the perfect escape hatch for the recommender to use. Signing your pre-created recommendation letter becomes not only the easy thing to do but also seemingly the right thing to do.

Despite what you might initially think, recommenders almost never take offense at a candidate's aggressive preparations (those that do can either be counted on to write wonderful recommendations without assistance or need to be reconsidered as potential recommenders). Instead, reactions are almost always the opposite: gratitude at making a tedious job easy and respect for a candidate's initiative and boldness.

Personal Experience

I utilized this methodology for obtaining recommendations during my second attempt at applying to law school. Of the three individuals from whom I requested recommendations (two professors and a work supervisor), two signed and submitted the recommendations that I created for them. The other one used my summary sheet to create a recommendation that was, if anything, slightly more effusive in describing my awesomeness than the recommendation I had previously prepared. In all cases, the recommenders were incredibly grateful for the preparatory work I did for them.

CHAPTER ELEVEN
OH NO, MY APPLICATION IS IN TROUBLE! HOW DO I FIX....?

Wow. Okay. So you have had your heart set on one particular school or maybe even a couple of schools, and for some reason your application is not up to snuff. Maybe you are already looking at a pile of rejection letters, or maybe you are looking at your cumulative GPA or your LSAT score and reading the handwriting on the wall.

What do you do now? Well, for starters just take a few deep breaths. It is all going to be okay. You have a couple of options. You can go to an alternate, equally awesome law school that *did* accept you. Maybe you would be happy there or maybe you could try to transfer to your dream school after your first year. A second option is to wait a year, attempt to improve your application in some way, and reapply to your dream school. A third option is to forego the idea of law school and pursue a different career all together.

I know it seems bleak, but before you head off to the airport to join the French Foreign Legion, let us take a moment to examine each option and see what choices you really have.

First Things First: Triage

Let's get a sense of the damage and see what is fixable. The questions you need to ask yourself now are, "What's the problem with my application?" and, "Do I even want to try to fix it?"

These are both the first and most important questions you need to ask. Figure out where the problem lies and then decide if it is worth pursuing. The answer is really going to dictate whether you give up on the idea of attending your dream school or possibly even give up on the idea of attending law school all together.

How do you find the problem? In the case of LSAT scores or cumulative GPAs, it should be pretty obvious. If either one are below the 25 percent marker for a particular school as listed on the U.S. News rankings, you should probably take that as a strong indicator. It might not be the only reason, but it is almost definitely a major factor.

What if both your LSAT score and GPA are solidly inside the 25-75 percent band for the school? In this case, the analysis now becomes a little more difficult. It is going to require some intuition on your part.

When I worked as an EMT on an ambulance during my time as a law student, I heard a saying often repeated by wizened old paramedics to their brash young EMT partners:

When you hear hoof beats, think horses not zebras.

This was usually the response to an EMT's convoluted diagnosis of, for example, a patient's migraine as a case of rare Dengue fever. It is really just a simpler way of describing Occam's razor, which is the theory of logic that states that all other things being equal, the simplest explanation is most often the correct one. For our purposes, you need to look at your application in its entirety and keep thinking about horses.

Ask yourself the following questions and see if you can judge the various aspects of your application with a more critical eye. If you cannot, maybe you can ask somebody else whose opinion you trust to look at it for you. Often, a third party's review of our work reveals problems, issues, and interpretations we never would have imagined.

— Do your grades have a substantial dip in them or do they trend downward?
— Is your undergraduate major or academic institution suffering from a reputation problem?
— Do you have any major flaws in the formatting of your application? For example, did you misspell the school's name or leave a reference to a different law school in your essays?
— Are your personal essays conveying the right information to the school? What about the right emotion?
— Have you given the school any reason, even inadvertently, to believe it was not your first choice?
— Are your recommendations good? Did a recommender not sufficiently recommend you?
— Was your application submitted outside of the school's admissions cycle? Did you break any administrative rules associated with the application process?

Any one of the issues mentioned above could potentially be enough to sink an otherwise suitable application packet. More likely, though, is that your application had multiple small-scale problems that cumulatively resulted in a denial of admissions. Go through it carefully or have someone you trust do it for you. Try to be as honest with yourself as possible.

Two Quick Tips

First, if you think it was your recommendation letters and you have already waived your right to read them, you can still go onto the LSAC and "deactivate" the letter. Get new recommenders. Read the recommendations before they are sent if possible. It seems like it would be socially awkward to ask your recommender to let you review their letter, but it really is not.

Second, if your favorite law school has sent you a rejection letter and, after going through the process described above, you remain completely stymied by the reason why, do not be afraid to call or e-mail the admissions office and simply ask them. Be professional and polite, but tell them that you are seriously considering reapplying in the following year and you want to make sure you address the deficiencies that hurt you this year. Tell them that you have examined your application and are unable to determine what the admissions committee found lacking. Thank them for their time and tell them that any guidance would be deeply appreciated.

Look, the worst thing that could happen is that they tell you that they can't help you. However, there is a really good chance that someone will treat your question with a measure of respect and review the admissions committee's internal notes. Regardless of the answer, be unfailingly polite. Certainly you may feel like telling the person on the phone to go soak their head for not picking you, but believe me when I say that the last thing you want to do is to let any animosity or petulance bubble to the surface. Even if the rejection sours your experience for now, you never know when you and that particular individual or school might cross paths again.

Potential Fixes for Application Problems

Now that you have a better sense of what your problems are, let's discuss options for mitigating them. The ideas listed below are certainly not the only choices you have available to you. They are just the ones that have worked for me or my friends and colleagues. Rehabilitating your application requires both your hard work and your creativity. If you think something will work for you, go ahead and try it.

1. If the problem is with your GPA

First, assuming you have been accepted at an alternate law school, you can attend your first year there. If you work very hard and dominate the first year academically, you will likely have a decent chance at a successful transfer application to your dream school. Fresh 1L grades are going to be substantially more relevant to a law school's admissions committee than an older undergraduate record.

Of course, there is also substantial risk. Most law schools utilize a grading curve that places the mean average grade of each course at either a B- or a B.

Depending on where you choose to attend and where you want to transfer, your curve-adjusted grades might not be up to snuff. In addition, the pool of transfer applicants nationwide is fairly large every year for popular and top-ranked schools, but the spots reserved for transfer students at each school are very limited. Lastly, you need to be careful that you do not jeopardize the financial aid package you have put together for the school you are currently attending.

Second, you can defer for a year and reapply. In the meantime, you need to improve your GPA somehow. How you choose to do that is up to you. Maybe you have time to declare a new minor before graduation or maybe the circumstances are such that you can audit classes for free. Many universities now offer a type of self-created masters program through their humanities and social sciences departments. In any case, delaying a year and taking classes offers two distinct advantages: it adds more time since you received your poor undergraduate marks and it also offers fresh evidence that you can succeed as a student at the collegiate and graduate level.

Personal Note

I knew when I decided to reapply to law school that I was facing a GPA problem. My first terrible attempt at college was weighing down the excellent academic record I built for myself after I returned to school. I decided to enroll in my university's graduate school as a self-directed masters' degree student. This meant I could design the degree around my own unique focus. The program was really intended to be for full-time professionals looking to specialize with studies relevant to their careers, but I was able to use it to substantially change my overall GPA and also to show that I could be successful at graduate-level academics.

I took one class in the following summer semester after deciding to delay law school for a year. I then enrolled in fifteen hours of coursework for both the fall and spring semesters, carefully focusing on my performance in each class I took. One year after my initial attempts to apply to law school, I submitted a new set of transcript records showing that I had accrued thirty-three additional credit hours with a GPA of 3.89. All of a sudden, my applications were a whole lot more competitive.

2. If the problem is your LSAT score

This issue is a little bit more challenging, if less time intensive, than the issue of a low GPA. The LSAT is a very difficult test, and as I have stressed earlier in this book, your chances of substantially improving your LSAT score are extremely low. If a bad LSAT score is your problem, then I strongly urge you to look at alternative schools...or an alternative career. That said, if your heart is absolutely set on tilting at this windmill one more time, then consider me to be your Sancho Panza.

You really only have one option here. You must pay for a commercial preparatory course. You must try to give yourself every physical and psychological advantage possible when the day of the test arrives. Eat well. Sleep well. As much as possible, make your preparation for the LSAT your central activity every day. Give yourself the maximum amount of time to prepare, and then go out and destroy the test.

Even though I like to think I have all the answers, I am still going to urge you strongly to research some of the very good LSAT preparatory books that are on the market. I am not just talking about books with old exams reprinted in them. The prep course you use should give you plenty of test questions. I am talking about the books that discuss methods for successful test taking such as always guessing (when you absolutely must guess) a particular letter because that letter has a slightly higher statistical average of being the correct answer than the other letters. The LSAT is a test of attrition. You need every advantage you can get.

3. If the problem is your personal essays

This is actually two separate issues. The first one is easy, though.

If your problem is that your personal essays are poorly written, then you need to rewrite your essays using a substantially increased level of care and consideration. It is very difficult, when you are emotionally invested in a piece of writing, to tell if it stinks or not. Once again, it is time to go find that person you trust. Take advantage of the time you have until you apply next year to carefully craft magnificent personal essays. Even bad writers can produce good writing with enough time, feedback, and work. Ask for criticism. Get help. Write fifty drafts. Write fifty more. Polish these essays into the gleaming gems they should have been the first time. You have, quite literally, all the time in the world. Go to it.

If your problem is that your personal essays lack depth, well that is a different problem all together. Fortunately, the problem is almost entirely in your head. So, once again, we need to determine the reason why. Is it because you lack (or think you lack) the sort of life experiences that your law school essay is trying to display? Is it because you are unsure of how to describe your dedication, qualification, or natural ability for the law?

Let me tell you a little secret: law schools have no idea what makes a good law student. Sure, they look for a certain level of academic training and an indication that you have the discipline to do the work, but when it comes to personality they have no preconceived notions of what makes a good law student versus a bad law student. They look, instead, for people who can show a sense of purpose or drive in their lives. Law schools do not want to believe that you are applying to them because you have run out of ways to delay graduation from college or because you failed out of medical school. They want to believe you have, on some level, felt a purpose in your life that makes the study of law necessary. Your job is to show that to them as best as you can.

How do you do that? Well, I think you need to start with a vision quest.

I know. You are thinking, 'Wait. What?'

What I mean is you need to get out of your own way and start thinking outside the box. One of the best ways to do that is to remove yourself from your comfort zone. Go camping. Go hiking. Go for a ten mile run someplace flat and straight and boring. Go sit on a rock and stare at the ocean. Go somewhere or do something where you can disconnect yourself from your day-to-day and look at yourself from the outside.

What makes you special? What makes you valuable? If you disappeared off the face of the earth tonight, who would miss you? Why? What is the purpose of your life? What is the purpose of life in general? What drives you forward?

As you ask yourself these questions, think about them in the context of law school. Is law school something you really need to do? If so, why? Can you turn that into an essay?

Once you get to that point, you are ready to write.

4. If the problem is the recommendations

Ooh, too easy. You are the master of your own ship, remember? Go get new recommendations. Follow my instructions in Chapter Ten. Tell the LSAC to deactivate or remove the old ones.

A Final Word

We have covered some tips and some tricks to help you rehabilitate a lackluster application, but I hope you take the time to really think about why you are reading this chapter. As we have discussed earlier, the law school application process should begin as a dispassionate and analytical assessment of your "best fit" schools. You are not just applying for admission to law school—you are applying for admission and financial aid.

Takeaway:

Falling in love with one particular school is a surefire way to end up with a broken heart and a lifetime of debt.

The sad reality is that if you are looking at ways to repair your application, it is most likely because you have already received a rejection letter. If so, it is almost impossible for you to go from rejected candidate one year to scholarship winner the next. Please, please, please reconsider your options.

CHAPTER TWELVE
MAKING YOUR FINAL CHOICE

My, what a long, strange trip it has been. You are almost at the end of your journey, which is, of course, the starting point for another, longer journey into the actual study of law. I hope you are excited because the time has come for you to pick your law school!

Let us review your timeline one last time.

It is now sometime in the spring semester. The snow has melted (or will melt soon) and the days are finally turning into the long, luxurious expanses of sun-drenched happiness that we all yearn for in the darkest parts of the winter. However, what is most important is that you are finally receiving your law school admissions letters. Now is finally the time to make your decision. Hopefully, this is a relatively easy process for you. If you were diligent about preparing and applying, you should have a variety of positive responses arrayed in front of you. It should be a simple matter of finding that sweet spot where the cost of attendance for each school intersects with your pre-determined level of mutual suitability and attraction. Then you just pick the school offering the biggest bang for the buck.

But first, let's address the issues of rejection and being waitlisted. It is my fervent hope that everybody reading this book achieved a substantial level of success in their law school applications. My hope is fervent, by the way, because I want you to leave good reviews about this book on Amazon and tell all your friends how awesome it is.

Please. Seriously. Help me sell a bunch of these things so I can pay off the ridiculously large student loans that I hope I have helped you to avoid.

Unfortunately, I also know that there will always be a few people for whom the process just was not what they needed it to be. For one reason or another, they find themselves looking at a series of rejection letters or notifications that they have been sent to the purgatory of the waitlist. You are not alone. I feel for you and I am here to help.

The Waitlist

In my personal opinion, being waitlisted is worse than being rejected. I think it stinks and you should think so too. At least when you are rejected, you know that the school is a dead end. You scratch it off your list and you move on. When you are waitlisted, you are added to the amorphous "maybe" pile where you can rot for months until the school finally rejects you or begrudgingly admits you.

Who needs that? Waitlisting is the academic equivalent of the law school having its cake and eating it too. Unfortunately, the only appropriate response from you is to do nothing. There is no upside to calling the school and telling them to go jump in a lake, and there is no downside to keeping your name on the list just in case. The emotional part of me would want to write a nasty e-mail to the admissions office just to tell them that I think they are a bunch of indecisive cowards, but the realist in me says I should fold the notification letter back into its envelope and set it aside for later.

On a positive note, if you were waitlisted at one school, it means you were very likely accepted somewhere else. Congratulations! However, if you do find yourself staring at the thin envelope in the mailbox, you should know your options. Let's discuss rejections.

Dealing with Rejection Letters

Rejection sucks. Nobody likes the feeling of somebody or something else out there simply not wanting them. It is even worse when it is academic rejection because you, the applicant, are basically asking the school if it wouldn't mind you paying it a tremendous amount of money to teach you a little something about the law...and the school basically says, "Nah. You're not good enough. Thanks anyway."

It is harsh. I know. All I can say is: They are wrong. They are flat wrong. I know it and you should know it. The school's decision to reject your application is not a reflection on you. It says nothing about your ability to succeed and it offers no evidence that you could not reapply next year and absolutely rock that school.

What it *does* say is that on the particular day that your file was reviewed, at the particular time that the committee met, and with that particular composition of that particular committee, the many things that were considered in weighing and measuring your application were not sufficient for the committee to extend you an offer of admission. Maybe the answer would have been different the day before and maybe it would have been different the day after. Nonetheless, on that day the answer was "no" and so it is time for you to move on.

Hopefully you have other schools to which you have been accepted. If so, take this rejection letter and stick it at the bottom of the pile. You do not need to worry about it ever again. However, if you fail to get accepted anywhere, then you should go back to Chapter Eleven and review your applications to identify the problem. All I can say is that it is not the end of the world. Find a way to make yourself productive for the next few months and try again next fall. You really can do it.

Takeaway:

One last point—and this one is really important: Do not ever allow a group of nameless, faceless people, whose highest achievement is that they work as bureaucrats for some law school, make you feel bad about yourself. Your worth and value in this world is totally unassociated with your law school applications.

Finding the Sweet Spot

So what do you do with your fat pile of acceptance letters? To start, you should call your friends and gloat. Just a little bit. You have accomplished something impressive here and you have the right to feel a little proud. Go ahead. You have earned it.

After you hang up the phone, take your list of schools and update it. Remove any schools to which you were rejected. Move all the waitlisted schools to the bottom of the list. In the end, you should end up with a list that reflects the preferentially-ranked schools to which you have been accepted.

Now draw a line off to the side of each school. On this line, write down how much you will need to borrow. How you choose to designate this is up to you. You can subtract scholarships and grants from the total cost of attendance (remember cost of attendance is the cost of tuition plus the cost of living) to get your number for your 1L year and then multiply this by three. If you do not want to attempt the math, you can make a notation like "Full scholarship; only borrowing living expenses" or "No scholarship; borrowing full amount" or "Half scholarship; In-state tuition."

What do you see? You have your list of schools that you want to attend and that have now indicated that they want you to attend as well, and you have the cost for you to attend each one. Does your best choice stand out? Among your list of possibilities, is there one that clearly meets that sweet spot between quality and cost more effectively than the others? I certainly hope so.

Personal Experience

The summer before law school, I was facing a mixed bag of success. I had applied to six schools and had been rejected from one, wait-listed at two, and accepted at three. In addition, I had applied to three "safety" schools and I was accepted into all three of them. These were not schools I was actually interested in attending so I disregarded their acceptance letters. Of my three "real" acceptances, I had a full ride scholarship offer to one school in California, no financial aid except federal and private loans to the second in Boston, and a 25 percent scholarship to the school I ultimately chose to attend – Vermont Law School. Why did I choose VLS? Almost a decade after making the decision, I think I have the perspective necessary to offer some insight into my decision-making process and why it was both the right choice and the wrong choice for me.

My GPA was a definite factor in the success of my law school applications. Although taking an additional year to pursue a master's degree and improve my overall GPA was a smart move, it still had only a moderate effect on improving my combined GPA. Plus, the many hours of poor grades I had received from my first college experience remained on my CAS Report. Although I could improve my cumulative GPA and show a trend of increasing maturity and scholastic achievement, I could not erase that horrible early transcript. I think that for some of my "reach" schools in the top 25 were turned off by that transcript. If you are top ranked law school and you had the choice of a student with great grades all the way through his or her career and a student with terrible grades and signs of a comeback, wouldn't you take the safe bet? I think my rejection school definitely took the safe best and possibly both of my wait-listed schools did as well.

So what I was left with were three acceptances. Not bad, given such a targeted search. I would have been happy attending any one of them. Why did I choose VLS? The short answer is that VLS was the safe middle ground. On paper, it seemed to split the difference between my three choices on issues of cost, quality, and happiness.

VLS offered a better financial aid package than my Boston choice, which wasn't offering any assistance, but it was not as good as my California school. While I probably would have borrowed an additional $20,000 to attend school in Boston, I would have only borrowed about $20,000 *total* to cover my cost of living that was not already covered by the scholarship in California. Still, as we have discussed previously, I had bought into the idea that an education was priceless. Who cares if I had to borrow to go to school? An education is never a bad investment, right?

VLS was ranked in the third tier, which is somewhere in the vast middle of the rankings, but it was also ranked number one in Environmental Law. My California choice was also in the third tier but had no specialty niche of which to brag. My Boston choice was ranked in the first tier, but it was not so highly ranked that I could guarantee heavy recruiter interest in me based just on the school's pedigree.

My thought was that I could carve out a specialty in environmental law and market myself as an environmental lawyer who attended the number one environmental law school in the country. My thought was to spin my alma mater like I had the choice of attending Harvard or Yale but I chose VLS instead because it was number one in my particular field of interest. To that end, incidentally, I did focus my law studies on the application and use of the Comprehensive Environmental Response, Compensation, and Liability Act (CERCLA). CERCLA is more commonly known as the Superfund law. If I hadn't found such a wonderful career in government doing what I love, I probably would be grinding out a living as an environmental lawyer in some state's or city's environmental regulatory agency.

Finally, in terms of happiness, VLS seemed to be the safe choice. It was close enough to be accessible to my wife's parents while far enough away from Boston that we would not be roped into every family function. California, on the other hand, was too far away. I had never visited it to know for sure that it would be a good fit. More importantly, my wife hated the idea of moving to California, and I knew that she would probably not stay if I forced the issue. So I chose VLS and I chose the financial aid package that came with it including the tens of thousands of dollars in loans I would need to borrow each year.

Hindsight is truly 20/20. If I knew then what I know now, I would have taken my California choice without a second thought. Of course, I could never have predicted the collapse of my marriage only a year and a half after moving to Vermont. I could never have understood the massive burden that my student loans represented. I could never have foreseen that my life would have taken the course that it has taken.

What I do know is that despite having a wonderful law school experience, my student loan burden has dramatically restricted the choices I have made and the practice of law I would have wanted to pursue. I know that the choices I make today continue to be influenced by my constant need to appropriately budget and plan for the payment of my loans. While this seemed an insignificant concern when I was a student, I can tell you that my perspective is radically different now that I am also trying to figure out how to budget and plan for my own children's future.

I loved my time in Vermont, but I have a feeling I would have loved my time in California as well. And if I could go back in time and whisper in my own ear, I would remind myself every day of about 130,000 additional reasons why I should choose California.

Making Your Choice

Frankly, I hope you have a school at the top of your list with a full scholarship offer. If you do not, then you have a choice to make: Which school and for how much debt? If that is the case for you, please permit me to give you one final piece of advice.

Law school is three years of your life. The minimum repayment period for student loans is ten years. Most students are forced by their economic reality to take a repayment period that lasts for thirty years. Ultimately, law school is just a means to an end: a short, three-year program that gets you a diploma and a ticket into the bar exam. The lawyer you become is far more a product of your own hard work and your own personality than any characteristics a particular law school can imprint on you in those short years. Do not waste your money. Take your list of acceptances and go where your cost of attendance is cheapest.

AFTERWARDS

YOU HAVE MADE your choice—Congratulations! Make sure you notify the school and send off your deposit check. You may now celebrate and buy a law school sweatshirt.

Make sure you stay focused as you finish your studies. It would be incredibly stupid to tank your final semester of undergraduate studies and actually put your acceptance or financial aid package at risk. Send off the final transcripts and make sure that all the paperwork that the law school needs from you and your previous academic institutions has been submitted.

This summer is going to be a busy time for you. You are transitioning from one part of your life to another. You will probably need to find new housing. You might even need to move across the country. Take the time to enjoy the little things right now because soon you will be too busy to notice. The first year of law school is a whirlwind of activity and it can be difficult to find time for anything not directly related to the pursuit of your studies.

There are several good books out there focused on preparing you for your first year of law school. I strongly encourage you to check them out and see if any of them resonate with you (at least, until I write a "how to prepare for your first year of law school" book). The first year is all about immersing yourself in the study of law. It will be very much like drinking from a fire hose. The time to learn how to read and brief a case and use a commercial outline is now. Do not wait until school starts in the fall. I did, and it resulted in my complete evisceration at the hands of my contracts professor on the third day of school. But that is a story for another time.

You are setting out on a whole new path. I wish you the best of luck and I hope you find the study of law to be as enriching and enjoyable as I did. You have a tremendous opportunity to do a great amount of good in the world. Let us see what you can do!

CPSIA information can be obtained
at www.ICGtesting.com
Printed in the USA
BVHW031121100219
539886BV00001B/81/P